# The New, Complete You

# Life Between

# —The Lines—

**BFG**
**Believe For**
**Greater**

To Kris
I pray that God will bless you in all you do. Believe in yourself & your gifts. Always be who God created you to be & You will always win!

*The New, Complete You*
by Justin Campbell

Additional editing by Carolyn Babione

For information, address:

The Church Online, LLC
1000 Ardmore Blvd.
Pittsburgh, PA 15221

International Standard Book Number: 978-1-940786-53-7

Library of Congress Catalogue Card Number: Available Upon Request

Printed in the United States of America

First Edition, March, 2017

**Trademarks**

## Dedication

I dedicate this book to my late brother's kids, Terry Campbell Jr. and Chris Campbell. (My brother, Terry Campbell, passed in 2009.) I also dedicate this to those I have mentored and still mentor, Amber Collins, Jared Griffith, Ray Hicks, and Lauren Camm. The joy I receive from seeing these young adults succeed and prosper is priceless. This is also for every child, teen, and young adult who has ever doubted who they are because of their situation or other people, yet made it or are trying to make it. I also thank God for all my family, friends, teachers, prayer partners, church members, coaches, pastors (Rev. Motley and Dr. Malone Jr.) for their spiritual covering and teaching that has gotten me where I am, and especially my father, Robert Campbell, and my mother, Teresa Couts, for raising me, believing in me, supporting me, and most of all bringing me up and teaching me about God and Jesus Christ! Lastly, I want to thank my beautiful and anointed wife, Tinika Campbell, who has been my biggest cheerleader. She is my rock, my Proverbs 31 woman, and we are truly one in Christ. I would be in trouble if I did not mention my wonderful and blessed girls, Jada and Mariah Campbell, and my stepdaughter, Ashlee Appleton. It is due to each of these fingerprints touching my life that I was able to write this book.

# SPECIAL THANKS

I would like to personally thank Allysan Corbett, a future 2017 graduate of New Albany High School, for helping me with the inspiration of my book cover! She sketched out and colored my ideas on paper, which led to the design of the book cover.

I would also like to thank my father, Bobby Campbell, for assisting with the reflection questions in each chapter. This helped me more than he knows.

I would like to thank my publisher, The Church Online, who has done a SUPERB job on this project. They have made publishing my first book stress-free by communicating well and being very professional.

# Focal Scripture of the Book:

Colossians 3:8-10 (NIV) says, "But now you must also rid yourselves of all such things as these: anger, rage, malice, slander, and filthy language from your lips.  Do not lie to each other, since you have taken off your old self with its practices and have put on the new self, which is being renewed in knowledge in the image of its Creator."

# Table of Contents

## Introduction

This book is for those who have parents, one parent, no parents, a guardian, a foster family, or ANYONE. In life, you will have choices that you have to make, and yes it helps to have the support of loved ones, but you can overcome and choose to live right regardless of your circumstances. You may be saying, "Justin, you do not know my circumstance." You are right; however, you still have a choice. You can choose to succumb to your circumstance or you can rise above it. Make up your mind today that you will be a success story and not just another victim. Yes, it may be hard, and you may have to make some tough decisions. You may have to leave some people behind, but in the end, you can say, "I MADE IT!"

*The New Complete You* deals with completion. In football, a completion is a forward pass that is caught in bounds. Complete means to bring to a finish or an end. Some other words or phrases that describe complete include all parts or elements, lacking nothing, whole, entire, or full. I know and believe that after you get done reading this book, you will be whole and will have the parts you need to stay in bounds and catch the FORWARD pass.

Between the lines of football, you must complete (yes, complete not compete, even though that is needed as well). You must complete that block, complete the pass, complete the run, complete the tackle, and complete the extra point. All this must be done within the boundaries of the rules of the game. Yet even after you complete all of this, there is a new chance to do it again and improve. Just as you complete plays in football, you also complete tasks and challenges in life. As you complete these tasks and challenges, you start to see some new characteristics in yourself that you did not know you had.

I pray that you enjoy this book about football, told through my eyes while undergoing the experience of playing in college. Even if you play or played another sport, you will be blessed by this book because every sport has coaches, tests, practices, and games. If you are in any leadership position, in a club, or on student council, this book is for you as well. I will use my own football experience and relate it to life. On a team, you must choose to believe in the coach and play for him/her. I pray that you will see that life can be as sweet as playing your favorite sport when you know who the true coach of your life is—GOD! If you play on His team, you will become an overcomer in EVERY area of your life. Just as becoming good in a sport is a process, becoming a good Christian and knowing Jesus Christ is also a process. You may have said, "I hate the place I am in" or "Everything is looking good." However, after reading this book you will be able to say, "I do not just feel good or brand new, but I feel COMPLETE!"

Enjoy the journey as I create a metaphor to link football and the Christian walk. While reflecting, take time to write your thoughts down in this book or in a notebook. Do not let this be just another book, but let this book push you to another place in your life. Every time you see a "Faith Walk" section, you are reading how the Christian process is like the process I went through in football!

> 2 Corinthians 5:7 (NKJV) says, "For we walk by faith [*believing*], not by sight [*seeing*]."

## CHAPTER 1 — START SOMEWHERE

### How I Got Started

Since the day that I scored my first touchdown in the fifth grade at St. Anthony's in Clarksville, Indiana, I knew that I wanted to play football in high school and then hopefully in college. As a junior high student, I was a very small guy in stature. What I lacked in size, I made up for with speed and heart. I remember my coach, Joe Theobald, always telling me, "Run north and south, rather than east and west." I understood what he meant, but I also saw a lot of guys trying to tackle me who were twice the size I was, which deterred me from running straight and trying to run towards the sideline to get around them. However, the first time I scored a touchdown and the crowd was screaming, the cheerleaders were cheering, my teammates were high fiving me, and my coach was praising me, I realized that running north and south was worth going up against players who were bigger than me. I realized that I wanted to play this sport as long as I could.

I continued my pursuit of football at Providence High School (PHS), where my first year I worked very hard in the weight room and studied hard to know the plays. I knew that if I studied, was attentive, and worked hard as a scout player (the guys who go against the starters), I would get a spot on the starting lineup. When we ran sprints, I tried to run faster than everyone. When they needed a player to fill in a spot, I jumped at the opportunity. I was always on time to meetings or practices so that the coaches knew I was serious about wanting to play. That year I was the mad dog (the player who went down on punt coverage) and a kickoff returner.

But just like anything, reaching your goals and dreams is not always that easy. That first year during double sessions, I severely sprained my wrist after another freshman fell on me after the play was already over. I remember that day vividly. As a matter of fact, it was one of the last plays of the day before we were to run sprints and practice would be over. I remember taking my shower with so many emotions flowing through my head. Would I be able to play that year? Would I lose my starting position? I even thought about how upset I was at the kid who fell on me because the play was over (he was not the most coordinated player, which made it worse). Fortunately, I was able to come back mid-season and ended up playing in the same two positions I mentioned above. When you work hard and have the right attitude, it really does pay off!

My second year at PHS I was the back-up for the running back and cornerback positions, and started as the kick returner and punt returner. Again, I worked very hard at all the things that I could control so that when my time came I would be prepared and the coaching staff would believe that I was ready. Unfortunately for him (but not so unfortunately for me), a player got hurt midway through the year, and the coaches started me at running back. I was excited, probably a little nervous, and shocked. I knew that I had worked hard, I was ready, I had paid attention in practice, and I knew the plays.

I was excited to finally get to show the coaches that I was ready and prepared to start a football game under the lights. It is so exciting to be out there on the field with the crowd cheering, your teammates encouraging you, the opponent taunting and threatening you, and the excitement of hearing your play called. I ended up having a very successful year and even shocked the coaches with my work ethic and moves. From that time on, I was the starting running back for the rest of my high school career and starting my junior year, I started at cornerback. Yes, you have it right, I played running back, cornerback, kick returner and punt returner by junior year!

## Choosing a College

The two sports that I was very good at were basketball and football. I started off playing basketball in high school because I liked it and I was good at it. After my sophomore season of basketball, I had decided that I wanted to play football in college. I had a great basketball career. My freshmen year we went 20-0 and my sophomore year we went 16-4. But I knew that I had to have two good years in football to impress the college coaches and I had to get bigger in order to be better. I then made the decision to stop playing basketball so that I could lift weights and work on more football-specific skills.

My dad supported me and sent me to Caritas, which was a sports acceleration training center to improve my form and speed. My senior year, comparing my body weight with what I was benching, I was the second strongest on the team and the fastest. I do not mention this as a pride issue, but I mention it to say that you must work hard to achieve your goals. To achieve your goals, it may mean that you have to give up some things and some time with friends, and instead spend more time sharpening your skills. I can tell you from experience that IT WILL PAY OFF!

After my senior year, my dad and I got some assistance with filling out college applications and sending out my information. Before I began applying, the first thing my parents and I did was look at the colleges that offered what I wanted to major in. I knew that I wanted to major in business marketing. Even if you do not know what you want to major in, there are other factors that you must consider.

First, you must ask yourself, "Do I want to go to school close to home or far away from home?" This is key because there is no point in looking at a school five hours away if you know that you cannot be that far away from your family. Second, you need to look at the school's graduation rate for athletes. To me, this is crucial because it lets you know that the

5

school cares about student athlete grades and not just about the talent of the athlete. Third, you need to look at the size of the school. A larger school means bigger class sizes and not necessarily as close of a personal relationship with professors as with a smaller school. Also, it is very easy to lose yourself and focus (values and beliefs) at a bigger school because of all the diverse activities and groups. I'm not saying you can't lose yourself at a smaller school; it is just easier to do at a larger school. As an athlete, the fourth thing you must do is check out the program of the sport you want to play: meet the coaches, talk to players, look at past records, and ask about the position you will be striving and fighting to earn. You should know that when coaches tell you that you will start for this or that position, it may change by the time the first game starts.

Remember, once you get to this level, most of the athletes are in the top of their class, so you must come in and show them that you really are the best person for that position. You must come in thinking that you are no higher than the second person on the depth chart so that you always work hard.

The last thing you must do is check out the campus and city life. If you want to join a fraternity/sorority, you should check them out. If you think that you may not return home after college, look at the city where the school is located. Does that city have job opportunities after you graduate and is it a city that you could see yourself living in? These were some of the things I thought about as I was looking at schools.

Now, I know I've listed a few important steps in choosing a college, but the two most important things to me were a great educational school and a great football program. I applied to nine schools and got accepted to all nine. A lot of that had to do with the fact that I finished high school with a 3.34 GPA. I am very proud of that, but I also could have done better. I would tell any student reading this book not to settle for less. Take that extra hour to study and go for more. I only realized this after being in college, and I do not want to see other students make the same mistakes. And I'm not just saying this. I just finished my Masters in Education in school counseling and received a 3.965 GPA. If you believe in yourself and set high goals, then it will translate into great results.

Now let me tell you that college applications are not all cake walks. Most applications require that you write a paper based on a question that they give you and each application also has a fee requirement. Because I wanted to play football, I chose to apply to more schools so that I could have choices in the end.

I also had to prepare a DVD to send to these football coaches so they could see if I would fit into their programs. I had to get the tapes of my senior year with times put on them, and pick the plays that showed my skill level. I gave my DVD a name, J.A.M., which meant Justin's Amazing Moves. You have the option of music and special graphics, but you should not pay the extra money for this because coaches are looking for talent, not design or music. I know I am showing my age because this is all done through the internet now.

After I sent my DVD to the nine schools where I got accepted, I reduced my choices to three: University of Tennessee (UT), Miami of Ohio, and Butler University (BU) in Indiana. The University of Tennessee was my favorite school to cheer for as I was growing up, so I looked up information on UT and sent a DVD to the school. I didn't mind being away from home, but I did not want to be too far away and UT fit my academic requirements. UT was the biggest school I looked at and I realized that even though it was a good school, it would be hard for me to play football there.

Miami of Ohio was the next school that I liked and I went to visit. Miami of Ohio has great academic programs and is ranked very high as a school. After attending an orientation session, I toured the campus. It was beautiful! I had missed the spring football game, but I did get to meet the coaching staff.

My father and I introduced ourselves and I began to tell them about myself and answered their questions. One of the coaches searched through a box about five feet in width and height for the DVD I had sent. A team can only have 105 people and the coach told me they already had 102 picked. The coach said, "I will call you and let you know if you will be one of the final three picked." So when my father and I left after talking to the coach and them not being able to find my video, I began to focus on my next choice, which was Butler.

Shortly after my visit to Miami of Ohio, I got a call from one of the Butler coaches. He apologized for not getting back to me sooner and said that they had gone through some coaching changes which was why I had not been contacted. The coach said, "I would really like to have you on our team," and then he proceeded by discussing how and where they would use me. After further investigation of the school, I realized it was comparable to Miami of Ohio. Butler is not very big, but it has a very beautiful campus and is ranked high academically. Despite its small size, Butler is located in a major city, Indianapolis, Indiana.

From this information, I'm sure you're thinking, *Justin, PICK BUTLER!* But that is not the whole story. After talking to my dad and praying, I chose BU. I called the coach and made a verbal commitment. The very next day the coach from Miami of Ohio called me and said, "I found your tape and we would like you to be on the team." As soon as I hung up I flew into my dad's office and said, "You will not believe who that was. That was Miami of Ohio and they want me to play for them." Even though I had verbally committed to BU, Miami of Ohio was originally my top choice. So my dad and I started to look further at the football programs. Miami of Ohio's program was in a better division, which meant more exposure. Butler, at the time, had a very high-powered offense which suited me well because I wanted to play offense. After we talked, my father said, "Well son, it is your choice. Pray and go where you feel God leading you."

I believe I took a day or two and that was all that was on my mind. As far as an education, I knew both schools had good academic programs so I was not worried about that. The tough part of the decision was the football team. I wanted to go somewhere that I could play and be effective, not sit on the bench. After much prayer and consideration, I ended up choosing Butler. Even though I felt God pushing me to Butler, I felt like I should have chosen the better football program at Miami of Ohio. Now that I have graduated, I am so glad I listened to God's guidance, because BU was truly where I was supposed to be. The saying is true, "Where God guides, He Provides!" And God provides for me EVERY time I need Him.

## Victory Testimony:

I met Justin in seventh grade when he became a coach for the junior high school team that I played on. I was around 13 years old and I thought that I was too cool for school. Right off the bat I knew that I was going to get along with him for multiple reasons. One, coming from a diverse background and being in a predominantly white atmosphere made it easier for me to get along with him because we could somewhat relate to the same things. He also had played the same position I did so he knew all about it. Two, it seemed that he genuinely cared about my success. My dad had coached football for 30 years so I was pretty good at picking out a coach who wasn't really interested, but Justin was not that coach. So, after my seventh grade year we began to work out together and he was getting me ready for the upcoming football season. For the first time, I learned what actual hard work was. I learned that I wasn't too cool for school and more importantly, grades were going to be much more important in the future than any sport-related endeavor that I would ever encounter. I was hardheaded so it definitely took some time to break my arrogant athlete mentality, but he stuck with me all the way through and it worked! I would like to think that I had a pretty good eighth grade year, and come high school I was ready. I was starting on the varsity team and I thought it was great. Coach Campbell had recently had a baby and could not coach anymore so it was weird not having him around keeping me in check, but he still always made an effort to reach out to me and see how I was doing. He was always trying to get me to come to church, which I appreciated because it showed he cared. As far as high school, my football career didn't pan out as I thought, due to the fact I was hurt every single year besides my senior year. It wasn't until my senior year when colleges began recruiting and the first thing they asked about every time was my grades that I truly received a reality check. My grades weren't so hot to say the least. Justin had always preached to me about how sports aren't everything. I ended up getting into a small college and tore my ACL the first day of practice and I gave up football after that. I transferred to Indiana University just to stick to getting an education and it is only now that I realize everything he has ever said to me has been right. If it weren't for Justin mentoring me through as a youth, I would say that I would not be the person I am today. He showed me that being humble is the right way and that making the grades is indeed extremely relevant. He taught me how to work hard, because that's the only way you are going to get the things you want in life, and in the end, it's worked out pretty well. Most of all, Justin taught me to think about my future, because the present can only take you so far.

—Jared Griffith

## REFLECTION

Every journey starts with one step. It does not have to be a big step, but a step of some sort. Ask yourself, "What is my next step?" Is it time for a new beginning or a new direction?

## FAITH WALK

➢ Psalm 34:8-10 says, "Taste and see that the LORD is good. Oh, the joys of those who take refuge in him! Fear the LORD, you his godly people, for those who fear him will have all they need. Even strong young lions sometimes go hungry, but those who trust in the LORD will lack no good thing" (NLT).

Just as I had to fill out college applications, you must try God and see that He is good. Just as I had to read and search on the internet about each school, you have to read and search in His word to learn and know about God. As you learn about His commandments and obey them, fear Him (this fear is awe or reverence), trust Him, and have faith, you shall not lack any good thing. Just think of the times that you trusted in a person and she or he failed you or let you down, which caused you trouble or grief. But God, who is not a man, will always come through for you.

➢ Numbers 23:19 says, "God is not a man, so he does not lie. He is not human, so he does not change his mind. Has he ever spoken and failed to act? Has he ever promised and not carried it through?" (NLT).

And because he owns time, HE IS ALWAYS ON TIME!

➢ Psalm 84:11 says, "For the LORD God is our sun and shield. He gives us grace and glory. The LORD will withhold no good thing from those who do what is right" (NLT).

In order to understand that God will not withhold any good thing from you, you have to try Him. Just like starting out in a sport for the first time, you do not know if you will like it until you stay with it until the end. When you were young, your parents put you in all kind of sports just so you would be active. After trying all of these sports, you decided that one in particular was the one you really liked. There were some sports for whatever reason that you decided you did not like. The awesome thing about God is that when you try Him and try Him with all of your heart and soul, you will see that He is good.

In any sport, your body and mind are going to go through some changes since it is something new. Practices will be hard. You will be disciplined. Coaches will yell, but it is all to get you ready for the game. The Christian walk is no different. Life will be tough. There will be tests. God will challenge you, but it is all so that you will be ready and stronger to represent Christ in the game of life. If God did not train you, you would fail the test later. But because we have gone through tests, we will know what to do when a circumstance arises, what to say in that circumstance, and we will be able to give God the glory for passing the test. Therefore, you must start by trying Him out, just as I tried running north and south, and you will see that He is good and He will accomplish what He says.

> Isaiah 55:11 says, "So shall My word be that goes forth from My mouth; It shall not return to Me void, but it shall accomplish what I please, and it shall prosper *in the thing* for which I sent it" (NKJV).

## Chapter 2 – Preparation

<u>Summer Workouts</u>

I got my first BU hat, signed my letter of commitment to Butler football in my high school gym, and my picture was in the evening news. I was officially a college football player at Butler University. I was very excited and thankful because a lot of people do not even make it to play in college. Well, that excitement got put on hold when I received a packet from the football coach. As I opened it up, out fell a workout program. My mouth dropped as I opened it and began to look it over. I realized that I was in the big leagues now and there was no more messing around.

The good news was that I had still been working out. Providence High School (in Clarksville, IN) allowed me to use the weight room and track. My father also paid for a program before I left called Sports Acceleration (in Louisville, Kentucky). The program was created to make athletes faster and better in their sport. They taught the basic fundamentals of running, strength training, and conditioning. I DEFINITELY RECOMMEND a program like this.

The summer workout was very detailed for each day. Even though I had previously been working out, the first three weeks were tough. Some may be thinking, *Did you actually do the whole workout?* And my answer is, "YES!" I was committed and determined to be in shape and come in ready to learn, work hard, and play. One thing that you must have is a mental toughness so you do not break when you are pushed because something is challenging. If I did not play, it was not going to be because I did not do my part, but rather because the coaches believed someone else was better. The other reason I did the workouts was because there was a test to pass when you first started training camp. I will discuss this further in Chapter Four.

I feel like you can learn something positive out of every experience you go through. As grueling as these workouts were, I could have stopped and made excuses, saying I needed to spend time with my family and friends or something similar. I didn't. This taught me that I had what it took to stay with something no matter the pressure or how difficult. The time that I gave up for what I loved doing was worth it when I ran across the end zone, passing that test. Even when things get tough or seem impossible, you have to find that inner strength to push through and believe that what is in you is great enough to get you through. If I am honest, writing this book has been tough. It is because of my trust in God's gifts and pressing through fear and worry that you are reading this book today!

## Leaving Home

Not only did I have to prepare for college by focusing on summer workouts, but I also had to prepare to leave family and friends that I was used to seeing all the time. I can't say I was entirely unprepared. My father made me go to camps when I was young, which I know to this day has made me the outgoing person I am, and I thank him for that. Some of the camps were sports camps and others were trade specific camps. Each camp lasted from three to five days.

When we got to camp, my dad would always make me introduce myself to other boys. I hated that. Now I am glad he did this. It is because of those experiences that I am able to introduce myself to anyone and could go to a school away from my family. Even though college would be for four years and not a week, I was used to leaving home and knew that we could visit each other whenever we wanted.

Leaving family was one thing, but leaving people that I hung out with every weekend and walked the halls with for 12 years was even tougher. When I went from seeing my best friends (Julie and Conley) five to six times a week, to knowing that it would be more like five times a year, that was rough on me.  I vividly remember Julie telling me, "You better not forget about me or replace me."  Little did she know there is no person in the world who could replace my Jules!

That first year was not too bad.  Julie came up a few times to visit and got to see me play a football game, and I saw her during my breaks.  It meant a lot that she came to my football game since she was one of my biggest fans in high school.  Conley and I were so close that his parents called me their other son.  Conley and I were usually at his house playing pool or basketball, or at Zesto getting a strawberry shortcake (I wonder if Conley remembers me making it there in five minutes from his house?).

My other two friends that I was leaving behind were Dominique and Gary.  Gary had gone to PHS with me, but ended up leaving and going to Jeffersonville High School.  However, we stayed in contact and he even came to visit me at BU.  Just like Julie, Gary was one of my biggest fans when it came to football.  I really appreciated him coming up to BU, watching my games, and hanging out with me.

Where do I even begin to describe my friendship with Dominique?  We went from playing against each other in sports and being rivals to being best friends.  Almost every weekend we were somewhere together: under 21 clubs, house parties, movies, driving down the strip, Catholic picnics, or hanging out with our Assumption High School crew (girls, you know who you are).  One of his friends, Donta, soon became my friend.  I called us "The Tripod" until Donta moved to Texas.  To this day, I thank God for these brothers because we all had the same characteristics: we didn't smoke weed, get drunk, smoke cigarettes, or act disrespectful.  With everything going on in the world, it is easy to get involved in other things, but I thank God we all had each other's backs and encouraged each other.

15

That summer before college was fantastic! I hung out with all my friends, realizing how important they were and how much I was going to miss them. At the same time, I was very excited to be adding another chapter to my life with this college experience. That summer, I worked so that I could have money while I was at college. I knew with football and school I would not have time for a job during the school year.

When you have true friends, they understand that you have to move on with your life and they won't make you feel guilty. Have you ever had someone try to make you feel guilty about a decision you made that was beneficial to your life? If so, that person did not have your best interest in mind, but rather was selfish and looking out for themselves. Friends should be loving and supportive of what will enhance you. Even though it hurt all of us because we would not be seeing each other as much, we knew that this was a part of the journey that had to take place. To this day, I still talk to Julie, Conley, and Gary, but I will admit not as much as I should. Dominique and I have stayed pretty close, too. When you have a family, it can get tough to get together with friends, but regardless of how much I see them, they will always be my true friends!

Then there were my parents, siblings, and extended family that I would miss. I would go from seeing my parents and sibling every day, and my extended family every Sunday after church for dinner, to just holidays. Even though I would miss the fun, food, and silliness, I was not the type of person that got homesick. You'll hear me say this a lot, but I truly thank God for my parents who instilled in me to work hard, be responsible, and be prepared. Always honor your father, mother, or guardian. I didn't always agree with everything they did or told me, but they are my parents and I knew I had to obey. It's like having a job. You don't always agree with your boss, but if you want to get a paycheck, you better respect them and do as they say. Parents will make mistakes, just as you will, but honor them because God has blessings for those who honor their caregivers.

I need you to fully understand just how important it is to make decisions that are the best for you. Of course it was difficult to leave my friends and family, but I had to better myself at college and pursue my dreams. I had to follow God's plan for me. Now, I can't say I was always the best at doing this. The summer after my first year of college, I came home to be with my family and friends. There was nothing wrong with this decision, but it was not what I needed to do. I wanted to be the best student and athlete I could be, so I took summer classes near my home at Indiana University Southeast to stay on track to graduate in four years. I worked out at home to stay in shape. I stayed on track, but in order to be in tip-top shape physically and mentally, I should have stayed at school where I had better resources. That alone is a spiritual lesson right there.

At Butler, I had a weight room when I needed it. I had a trainer. I had medical trainers. I had coaches there who could assist me and get me to where I needed to be. I also had other veteran players there to give me their wisdom. Sometimes in life, you have to make decisions that don't seem like a big deal, but can change and shape who you are and affect your destiny!

The next two summers, I stayed at school and boy did I see a difference. You have to be able to learn from past mistakes and move forward, rather than let the past hold you back from your future successes. I saw a difference in my speed, agility, strength, and knowledge of the game. Who knows what would have happened had I stayed at school that first summer? Now, I take time to think about my choices a little more and how they can affect me. There comes a time when you have to stop worrying about others and focus on you. This may mean making a difficult decision to leave family and friends as I did. But trust in God; there is no failure in Him. Do not be afraid to try new experiences because that is when you discover great things about yourself you never would have known had you not taken that first step of faith!

---

**Victory Testimony:**

Justin has played an influential role in my life for many years now, no matter how long it's been since we last saw each other. After I went away to school, we became somewhat distant, but the encouragement never ceased. I first met him during my sophomore year in high school as he was the director of a youth group I joined. I was immediately drawn to his personality and the atmosphere he created each time we met. It was always refreshing to see him because I knew a warm hug and encouraging words would surely follow. It didn't take long for Justin to become one of the most important people in my life, and he graciously accepted the role. He was like a father, a best friend, a coach, and a mentor, all in one. Our daily conversations helped me to grow exponentially not only in life, but in my spiritual walk as well. I was raised in the church, but I drifted away for a few years. Justin grabbed my hand and led me back, literally. He provided the testimonies, experiences, and encouragement that reminded me why I fell in love with God to begin with. Justin always held me accountable, and that was exactly what I needed to get back to where I was before and continue to grow. Even today, I haven't talked to Justin in a few weeks, but I've never forgotten what he has taught me. The lessons and love I took from our relationship still has a prominent role in my daily life.
—Amber Collins

---

## REFLECTION

Now that you have taken a step, you need to get ready. Preparation requires action. What do you need to take another step? Who do you need to talk to? Who do you know that is taking the same steps you are taking?

## FAITH WALK

I had to prepare to leave home and friends for a greater purpose: higher education. As you start your journey with God, you must prepare so that you will be equipped. First, you must know the word of God.

> ➤ 2 Timothy 2:15: "Work hard so you can present yourself to God and receive his approval. Be a good worker, one who does not need to be ashamed and who correctly explains the word of truth" (NLT).

The first two words say, "Work hard!" This is not the kind of studying where you skim, but rather where you give God quiet and undivided time. It's like the playbook. If you do not study it, you will not know the plays. The same is true of God's word; if you do not read it, you will not know when He is giving you directions. God will be telling you to take a time out, but you cannot hear him because you are trying to run a two-minute drill—busy and moving at a faster pace than God. Just listen to these two passages of scripture:

> ➤ Psalm 119:105: "Your word is a lamp to guide my feet and a light for my path" (NLT).
> ➤ Proverbs 3:5-6: "Trust in the Lord with all your heart, and lean not on your own understanding; In all your ways acknowledge Him, and He shall direct your paths" (NKJV).

As you understand the Word, it will reveal how to live a godly life and expose our rebellion. When you play a sport, whether football or something else, as you start to train and study the playbook, you realize what you are great at and what you need improvement on.

> ➤ 2 Timothy 3:16: "All Scripture is inspired by God and is useful to teach us what is true and to make us realize

what is wrong in our lives. It corrects us when we are wrong and teaches us to do what is right" (NLT).

The Bible is no different. It will help you to become more like Jesus every day if you will choose to apply and practice what you read.

Finally, once you know the word, you must practice it so that you can receive the reward or promises that God has for you.

> 1 Timothy 4:7-8: "Do not waste time arguing over godless ideas and old wives' tales. Instead, train yourself to be godly. Physical training is good, but training for godliness is much better, promising benefits in this life and in the life to come" (NLT).

Just as you would train and practice to win regular season games in hopes of making the tournament and winning it all, you should want to train to win the spiritual promises of God. In the same way you lift weights, run, and punish your body physically, you should also read, pray, and punish your body spiritually. All the muscles in the world will not help a sick family member. All the money in the world will not help low self-esteem. But the God who created you also knows you and can bless you with things that are spiritual, lasting, and eternal!

> Ephesians 1:3: "All praise to God, the Father of our Lord Jesus Christ, who has blessed us with every spiritual blessing in the heavenly realms because we are united with Christ" (NLT).

> Matthew 6:19-21: "Don't store up treasures here on earth, where moths eat them and rust destroys them, and where thieves break in and steal. Store your treasures in heaven, where moths and rust cannot destroy, and thieves do not break in and steal. Wherever your treasure is, there the desires of your heart will also be" (NLT).

The key is to love the things of God. As you study and learn what God loves, His desires will guide your actions. But if you never take the time to read the Bible and only focus on what you hear, you will do what you want and what pleases the flesh. However, the monetary and material gains like clothes, money, shoes, video games, etc. will all fade away or perish. Showing love, helping others, caring for people, and forgiving others are the godly desires that will last.

## Chapter 3 — Anticipation

### Finally at Butler

As I have grown up, I have always taken things in stride. I never expected I would be a college football player, but I had the right people around me who pushed me to put in the hard work and practice, and I was blessed (or fortunate enough) to get the chance to play. My first big moment that I had to take in stride came for me in mid-August when I stepped onto Butler's campus for the first time. It was a beautiful summer day and the campus was pretty quiet. A lovely neighborhood surrounded the campus and the flowers and trees just made it perfect!

*YES! I am officially a collegiate student athlete,* I thought.

As my parents and I drove onto the campus, we were looking for the dorm where I would stay, Ross Hall. When we found Ross Hall, sitting out front were a few coaches, resident assistants (RAs), and a few volunteers to help me move in. I was so excited to finally be at college and start the journey. Immediately, I started meeting people, talking to the coaches, and yes, checking out a few of the RAs.

So, I got my room key and found my room. I thank God that my room was on the first floor and not the second floor or in the basement. I can't even imagine having to carry everything I brought up and down the stairs. My roommate, Adam, graduated with me at Providence High School.

### Football Orientation

After I got settled in, activities started right away. There was a meeting to give parents general information about what would take place. We discussed buying apparel, the away games, and where we would stay, and paperwork that needed to be signed. You had a little time to go back and finish unpacking and then say your goodbyes to parents. It was sad, but at the same time, I knew my parents would be at every game. I saw them every Saturday for the first three months of college. At the time, I wondered how they felt that first day going back home. My mom said that dad cried a few nights, but that has not been confirmed.

Next, I had a team meeting with everyone. I vividly remember walking into that room for the first time and seeing all the upperclassmen. Some of the guys were just big—muscles bulging. They were sizing me up, and I must say, it was a tad bit intimidating. After the team meeting, we were grouped by our positions. All the upperclassmen had rapport with each other and were making remarks under their breath. I knew that I was going to have to work hard and let my work ethic do the talking. With my outgoing personality, I knew I was okay there, but with these guys, charm was not going to do it.

The next day was more exciting because it was the day we got our football pads and lockers. My adrenaline was rushing. The locker room was pretty big and there was a bulldog in the middle of the carpeted floor, a big shower room with a music system, and a weight room connected to our locker room. The best part was the tunnel you got to walk out of for every game!

After getting my pads, shoes, practice pants, and jerseys, we had our first true football meeting. At the meeting, the first thing we received was the playbook. Keep in mind, I was a running back in high school and that is what I wanted to be in college. When I got to campus, the coaches wanted to use my talent and speed and get me on the field right away. They did not need running backs and wanted me to be a receiver or a defensive back. I reluctantly chose receiver. So, the playbook had pages and pages of plays that I had to learn for a position I was not accustomed to. At first glance I thought, *There is no way,* but as each day progressed, I learned more and more.

The first days were filled with meetings and preliminary details. Little did I know that in a few days the dorms would get a little bit more fun. Shortly after the football players arrived on campus, the soccer and volleyball team arrived for double sessions. The campus was not only starting to feel a little more like college, but now there were some ladies on campus! After a while you get tired of just seeing guys. With my personality, it did not take long for me to get to know some of the soccer and volleyball girls.

So let me set this picture up: the first semester we ended up bunking our beds so that we would have more space. I had a program where you could download music, so attached to my computer were speakers and a mid-size subwoofer. Above my door, I had cut-out letters that spelled out "Club Sweetness." A backlight hung under my roommate's bed; my bed was on the bottom. I know my sister and her friend, Kim, are probably laughing as they read this, recalling past conversations.

So as you can see, my room was set up pretty nice and it became the hangout spot during double sessions. We would all relax and watch movies, talk about practice, and discuss our excitement for our first games. The time we all spent was much-needed after a brutal day of sweating in the sun and long chalk talks (team meetings about plays). I know some of you want to know, so yes, there were some fine, fine girls on the soccer team and some toned, long-legged girls on the volleyball team. It was a 3:1 ratio girls to boys on campus.

## REFLECTION

When you take the proper action, you should have expectation. What do you expect after the steps you have taken? You may not know what to anticipate yet, but keep on stepping because it will come.

# FAITH WALK

Now that you have started preparing to be a Christian and are seeing the changes that must be made in your life, you need to be saved. The brutal truth is that this walk is impossible without the Holy Spirit, so salvation is vital. (Now if you are already saved, keep reading because this section may help you to take someone else through the plan of salvation.) Just as I anticipated meeting new friends and coaches, you will anticipate the day you can say, "I am saved and I have unspeakable joy" or "I have led someone to Christ."

The plan to salvation means you must realize that everyone has sinned except Jesus. Sin entered the world because the first man, Adam, willfully disobeyed God (Genesis 2:15-3:24, NLT). It is important to realize that God had spoken to Adam, but Eve was deceived by the serpent.

> ➢ Romans 6:23: "For the wages of sin is death, but the free gift of God is eternal life through Christ Jesus our Lord" (NLT).

So for us to get back to a right relationship with God and to get rid of the effects of sin, we must be saved.

> ➢ Romans 3:23-24: "For everyone has sinned; we all fall short of God's glorious standard. Yet God freely and graciously declares that we are righteous *[justification]*. He did this through Christ Jesus when he freed *[redemption]* us from the penalty for our sins" (NLT).

So now that you realize there is a God who has a game plan for justifying you and declaring you not guilty, you must confess.

> ➢ Romans 10:8-10: "In fact, it says, 'The message is very close at hand; it is on your lips and in your heart.' And that message is the very message about faith that we preach: If you openly declare that Jesus is Lord and believe in your heart that God raised him from the dead, you will be saved. For it is by believing in your heart that you are made right with God, and it is by openly declaring your faith that you are saved" (NLT).

➢ John 3:16-18: "For this is how God loved the world: He gave his one and only Son, so that everyone who believes in him will not perish but have eternal life. God sent his Son into the world not to judge the world, but to save the world through him. There is no judgment against anyone who believes in him. But anyone who does not believe in him has already been judged for not believing in God's one and only Son" (NLT).

One thing that is very important to note is that your good deeds will not save you. If you were saved by your good works, this would cancel out the grace of God (Jesus' death on the cross and resurrection). Because we all have the capacity to sin, I am glad that it is not by works, because that means you could do wrong and work your way out of being saved, which is not the case.

➢ Ephesians 2:8-10: "God saved you by his grace when you believed. And you can't take credit for this; it is a gift from God. Salvation is not a reward for the good things we have done, so none of us can boast about it. For we are God's masterpiece. He has created us anew in Christ Jesus, so we can do the good things he planned for us long ago" (NLT).

When a coach calls a play, he has to plan on how it will be successful as well. In football, when the coach calls for a pass play, he has to have enough men to block and protect the quarterback so that he can throw the ball. And when you become saved, God does not leave you helpless. When you accept Christ as your Lord and Savior, the Holy Spirit comes to live in you and guide you.

➢ Romans 8:11: "The Spirit of God, who raised Jesus from the dead, lives in you. And just as God raised Christ Jesus from the dead, he will give life to your mortal bodies by this same Spirit living within you" (NLT).

You have probably heard people say that they have messed up so bad that they cannot go back to church or that they are not saved anymore.

> Ephesians 1:13: "And now you Gentiles have also heard the truth, the Good News that God saves you. And when you believed in Christ, he identified you as his own by giving you the Holy Spirit, whom he promised long ago" (NLT).

Remember that this is why you got saved—to receive the comforter, the Holy Spirit. We all sin and will continue to sin even once we are saved. Because you are saved, you now have forgiveness of sin. Because of your right relationship and because of the help of the Holy Spirit, you will want to do the work of Christ instead of the work of self. You have realized you cannot do it on your own. You need the one who created you to order your steps and as you do, you will sin less and less.

> James 3:13-18: "If you are wise and understand God's ways, prove it by living an honorable life, doing good works with the humility that comes from wisdom. But if you are bitterly jealous and there is selfish ambition in your heart, don't cover up the truth with boasting and lying. For jealousy and selfishness are not God's kind of wisdom. Such things are earthly, unspiritual, and demonic. For wherever there is jealousy and selfish ambition, there you will find disorder and evil of every kind. But the wisdom from above is first of all pure. It is also peace loving, gentle at all times, and willing to yield to others. It is full of mercy and the fruit of good deeds. It shows no favoritism and is always sincere. And those who are peacemakers will plant seeds of peace and reap a harvest of righteousness" (NLT).

Just as you learn the playbook on a team, you are now part of an elite team called Christian. Your playbook is the Word of God or the Bible. As you read and study the word of

God, it speaks to the Holy Spirit within you and then guides you in your life.

> John 14:15-17: "'If you love me, obey my commandments. And I will ask the Father, and he will give you another Advocate, who will never leave you. He is the Holy Spirit, who leads into all truth. The world cannot receive him, because it isn't looking for him and doesn't recognize him. But you know him, because he lives with you now and later will be in you" (NLT).

> John 16:13-14: "When the Spirit of truth comes, he will guide you into all truth. He will not speak on his own but will tell you what he has heard. He will tell you about the future. He will bring me glory by telling you whatever he receives from me" (NLT).

As I've said before, the amazing thing is that God is not a man and cannot lie, so as you study the word and you are guided by the Spirit, you can trust that God will lead you the right way.

Not only will the Holy Spirit lead and guide you, but it will enable you to do great things.

> John 14:12-14 says, "'I tell you the truth, anyone who believes in me will do the same works I have done, and even greater works, because I am going to be with the Father. You can ask for anything in my name, and I will do it, so that the Son can bring glory to the Father. Yes, ask me for anything in my name, and I will do it!" (NLT).

With power comes responsibility! You are not given the Holy Spirit as if it is magic, or for personal gain, but you are given the Spirit to bring glory to God. That is why the last verse says "anything you ask in my name," which means in Jesus' name. So in order to know what will bring God glory, you must read His word and pray so that your spirit knows what to ask. If you are a player on a team, the only way you know what play to call is by reading and studying the playbook. The same is true with the word of God. As you read the Bible, the Holy Spirit will tell you the things you need to do throughout your day to give God glory and the only way you know what to do daily is to read the word of God daily.

You have to read daily because you may be calling "Play One," again when God is trying to tell you "Play Two," because "Play One" will not work for this problem. The wonderful thing about God is that He is so great that you will never be able to fully have a handle on Him, yet He will show you more about Him on a continual basis. Remember this: Jesus healed people, fed people, was kind to the poor, and served others; He tells us that we will be able to do this and more because the same power that He had is now in us, through the Holy Spirit.

Now that you know how to become saved, you understand the purpose of the Holy Spirit, you know that you are to give God glory with your life, and you understand that grace is a free gift, we will finally look at how you should feel about yourself. You may have been told you would be nothing and will amount to nothing. You do not have to believe that because God is pleased with everything He creates. So before you became saved, God was pleased with you, and now that you are saved let us look at what God's word says about you and how He is still pleased with you.

➤ Psalm 139:13-18: "You made all the delicate, inner parts of my body and knit me together in my mother's womb. Thank you for making me so wonderfully complex! Your workmanship is marvelous—how well I know it. You watched me as I was being formed in utter seclusion, as I was woven together in the dark of the womb. You saw me before I was born. Every day of my life was recorded in your book. Every moment was laid out before a single day had passed. How precious are your thoughts about me, O God. They cannot be numbered! I can't even count them; they outnumber the grains of sand! And when I wake up, you are still with me!" (NLT).

➤ Genesis 1:26-31: "Then God said, 'Let us make human beings in our image, to be like us. They will reign over the fish in the sea, the birds in the sky, the livestock, all the wild animals on the earth, and the small animals that scurry along the ground.' So God created human beings in his own image. In the image of God he created them; male and female he created them. Then God blessed them and said, 'Be fruitful and multiply. Fill the earth and govern it. Reign over the fish in the sea, the birds in the sky, and all the animals that scurry along the ground.' Then God said, 'Look! I have given you every seed-bearing plant throughout the earth and all the fruit trees for your food. And I have given every green plant as food for all the wild animals, the birds in the sky, and the small animals that scurry along the ground—everything that has life.' And that is what happened. Then God looked over all he had made, and he saw that it was very good! And evening passed and morning came, marking the sixth day" (NLT).

➤ Psalm 8:4-5: "What are mere mortals that you should think about them, human beings that you should care for them? Yet you made them only a little lower than God and crowned them with glory and honor" (NLT).

Not only were you fearfully and wonderfully made, but God is mindful of you and created you in His image and likeness. Yes, the God who created the world and has all power created you in His image and likeness! That should make you smile and be excited about what is to come in your life as a Christian. Now say this verse out loud and believe it:

"I CAN DO ALL THINGS THROUGH CHRIST WHO STRENGTHENS ME" (Philippians 4:13, NKJV).

30

This is a great scripture to declare on a regular basis and to remind you that it is not by your own strength, but by Christ's strength that is in you through the Holy Spirit that you can make it through every trial, situation, dilemma, heartache, and financial struggle.

---

Our Deepest Fear
*A Poem*
By: Marianne Williamson

"Our deepest fear is not that we are inadequate. Our deepest fear is that we are powerful beyond measure. It is our light, not our darkness that most frightens us. We ask ourselves, Who am I to be brilliant, gorgeous, talented, fabulous? Actually, who are you not to be? You are a child of God. Your playing small does not serve the world. There is nothing enlightened about shrinking so that other people won't feel insecure around you. We are all meant to shine, as children do. We were born to make manifest the glory of God that is within us. It's not just in some of us; it's in everyone. And as we let our own light shine, we unconsciously give other people permission to do the same. As we are liberated from our own fear, our presence automatically liberates others."

---

Choose in your mind and in your heart to be the best student, the best child, the best person you can be every day, REGARDLESS of what others do or say. Remember, you have the power and it is your choice! A quote I often read says, "Show respect even to people who don't deserve it, not as a reflection of their character, but as a reflection of yours" (Dave Willis).

## CHAPTER 4 — THE PRE-TEST

For one day, or better yet, for one hour, all the fun came to a halt. I had my first test and I had only been on campus for half of a week. It was not a school test. It was a 300-yard shuttle run test that measured the amount of work we put in during the off season. Each position had a time they had to beat to pass. Of course, the skill positions, which I played, required the quickest times. The test consisted of two 300-yard sprints and was broken down into five 60-yard sprints with a minute break, then five more 60-yard sprints. The two times had to average below what your position time was or there were consequences, like waking up early every morning for one or two weeks to run.

It was one of the hottest days and the sun was blazing. Almost every player ran with a girdle on where your hip and butt pads go. I was in the second or third group and even though I had worked hard all summer, I was unsure of how I would do. People were finishing with cramps. Some could barely catch a breath, and others threw up. While watching everyone else, I figured that I better come up with some kind of strategy. So, I decided that every other time I turned to run the other way, I would ask my time keeper for my time. This way I would know if I needed to dig in deeper and pick up my speed.

When it was my turn and I first started, I thought, *This is not too bad.* Then after the fourth turn I thought, *Okay I feel it a little now, but I will get a minute break, so on this last lap let's push it a little harder.* I made great use of my break. I drank A LOT of water, stretched, and asked my time. I am not 100% sure, but I believe my time was around 46 or 47 seconds. For my next turn, my time keeper counted me down to start again by saying, "3, 2, 1," and off I went. This round was much harder. By the time I got midway through the third lap, I was feeling it. I thought my stride was good, but when my time keeper said my

32

time, I had to find something inside me to push through the pain. There is a lesson in that sentence. I got to my last lap and I was close to where I needed to be. With all the players yelling and encouraging those of us that were running, and with my will to succeed, I found another gear in that last lap even with my legs being tired and my breathing heavy. THANK YOU GOD!

At first when I finished, I did not care about my time because I was so tired, thirsty, and sore. I just wanted to lie in the grass, but the trainers made us walk around. It is not good for your legs to stop moving after that much running. My time keeper gave both of my times to the coach, and when I finally caught my breath, I was eager to see my times. You know how I said that I was close on the last lap? If I had not found that power from within me to push, I would not have passed. I PASSED, and I passed by tenths of a second. My two times were averaged, and I was so close that my overall time was rounded down.

Spiritually, there are so many lessons from that test. But don't worry, I'll delve into those a little bit later! Buckle up, because it is about to get real good!

## REFLECTION

You have taken a step. You are prepared. Your anticipation is rising. Yet, get ready because as you move forward you will be tested. What test are you going through right now (family, friends, sport, job, etc.)? How can your test make you stronger? Whatever the test, DO NOT STOP, because victory is right past the test.

## FAITH WALK

When you think of tests, a lot of times you give them a negative connotation. You hate to study. You dislike the time it consumes, and you hate waiting for grades. You do not like the pre-test even though it lets you know where you are and what you need to do to get where you are going. Whatever you feel about tests, God's tests are not to destroy you (that is the enemy and his temptations), but to DEVELOP you! You can be assured that God will send tests your way.

> Psalm 7:9-10: "Oh, let the wickedness of the wicked come to an end, But establish the just; For the righteous God tests the hearts and minds. My defense *is* of God, Who saves the upright in heart" (NKJV).

These verses let you know that He tests your heart and mind. Your ideas will take root in your heart, and will be revealed through your actions. God is testing you to develop you into the Christian you need to be. As an athlete, you may come in playing one position, but the coach may see that you would be more useful at another position. And as a person, God knows who He created you to be, but he has to change your thinking from the world's view (the devil's territory) to a Christian view so that you may be useful in the Kingdom of God.

Let's look at Job's test in the Bible.

> Job 1:8 says, "Then the Lord asked Satan, 'Have you noticed my servant Job? He is the finest man in all the earth. He is blameless—a man of complete integrity. He fears God and stays away from evil" (NLT).

The first thing you see is that the Lord asked Satan because God knew Job would pass the test. One thing you must realize as a Christian is that trials and bad circumstances will happen. Some of these trials will be tests from God himself and some are just random occurrences. However, what gives you confidence as a Christian is that God has all power and knows what is going to happen before it comes into your life. And because He allowed it to happen and already knew what was going to happen, He has a solution already figured out. This is where your faith comes into existence.

As an athlete, you may not always understand why you have to do some of the drills you do. But at some point in the game, you may find yourself using the very skill that was taught to you in practice. As Christians, you may encounter someone who is going through what you have already experienced and now you are able to encourage this person about how God brought you through. Or, in the midst of the situation, you find out that you have an issue of pride, trust, forgiveness, or some other issue and now your faith is stronger and you are able to depend on God more! The key is that you will make it through. Through means in one side and out another, or completion. Know that, just like you made it through double sessions and through those drills, as a Christian you will make it through every trial to completion because God is with you!

> John 16:33: "I have told you these things, so that in Me you may have [perfect] peace. In the world you have tribulation *and* distress *and* suffering, but be courageous [be confident, be undaunted, be filled with joy]; I have overcome the world [My conquest is accomplished, My victory abiding]" (AMP).

> Matthew 1:23: says, "'Behold, the virgin shall be with child, and bear a Son, and they shall call His name Immanuel,' which is translated, 'God with us'" (NKJV).

So God knew Job would pass the test because it tells us in the scripture.

> Job 1:1 says, "There was a man in the land of Uz whose name was Job; and that man was blameless and upright, and one who feared God [with reverence] and abstained from *and* turned away from evil [because he honored God]" (AMP).

You will always pass the test when you fear God and abstain from evil. The way to do this is to read the word of God which gives you strength and wisdom. Will you be perfect? No. But even when you stumble, you will stumble forward for a first down!

During Job's test, he lost his children, livestock/animals, his job, and his health. His wife and friends thought it was due

35

to some sin he had committed. In spite of all that happened and after receiving advice that he should just curse God, Job never does. He does ask God some questions about why he is suffering, though. God never answers Job about why he is suffering, but God does ask Job a series of questions. Sometimes it is not for you to know why it happens, but to simply trust God.

> Job 23:10: "But he knows where I am going. And when he tests me, I will come out as pure as gold" (NLT).

If you will do your part by trusting and having faith, God will ALWAYS do his part just as he did with Job. You see this fulfilled when you read Job 42:10, which says:

> "When Job prayed for his friends, the Lord restored his fortunes. In fact, the Lord gave him twice as much as before!" (NLT).

You have to realize that God is faithful even when you are not, but sometimes a blessing does require your participation (which means obedience, prayer, and forgiveness, or whatever God tells us).

> 2 Timothy 2:13: "If we are unfaithful, he remains faithful, for he cannot deny who he is" (NLT).

As a teenager or person maturing in the Lord, you must realize that God's test helps you learn patience and must be seen from a divine or spiritual perspective now that you are saved.

> Isaiah 40:29-31: "He gives power to the weak, And to those who have no might He increases strength. Even the youths shall faint and be weary, And the young men shall utterly fall, But those who wait on the Lord Shall renew *their* strength; They shall mount up with wings like eagles, They shall run and not be weary, They shall walk and not faint" (NKJV).

> Romans 8:26-27: "And the Holy Spirit helps us in our weakness. For example, we don't know what God wants us to pray for. But the Holy Spirit prays for us with groanings that cannot be expressed in words. And the

Father who knows all hearts knows what the Spirit is saying, for the Spirit pleads for us believers in harmony with God's own will" (NLT).

You need to know that all suffering is not because of sin. Sometimes God permits you to suffer so he can move you closer to Him and to develop your character so it will be more like His. Just like Daniel and the three Hebrew boys (**see Daniel 3:13-30, NLT**), God can allow you to be put in a fire and because He has his covering around you, you won't be burned, yet you will come out looking better than when you went in.

> ➤ Psalm 84:11: "For the Lord God is our sun and our shield. He gives us grace and glory. The Lord will withhold no good thing from those who do what is right" (NLT).

> ➤ Psalm 91:2-4: "This I declare about the Lord: He alone is my refuge, my place of safety; he is my God, and I trust him. For he will rescue you from every trap and protect you from deadly disease. He will cover you with his feathers. He will shelter you with his wings. His faithful promises are your armor and protection" (NLT).

Lastly, after we ran our 300-yard shuttle test, if we did not make our times there were some consequences. God is the same way. We love His mercy and grace, but at times we hate His correction. I thank God that He pulls me back in and closes doors I do not need to walk through. I thank God that He humbles me and takes some possessions or decisions back because I was too proud or hardheaded. Sometimes God has to humiliate you to get humility in you. Prayerfully, you will get to a place where you can bless the Lord at all times, good or bad!

> ➤ Psalm 34:1: "I will bless the Lord at all times; His praise *shall* continually *be* in my mouth" (NKJV).

Regardless of what happens, good or bad, I know I am okay because I am the Lord's and He takes care of His children.

- Romans 14:8: "For if we live, we live to the Lord; and if we die, we die to the Lord. Therefore, whether we live or die, we are the Lord's" (NKJV).
- Psalm 37:25: "I have been young, and *now* am old; Yet I have not seen the righteous forsaken *[abandoned],* Nor his descendants *[children/seed]* begging bread" (NKJV).
- Psalm 34:10: "Even strong young lions sometimes go hungry, but those who trust in the Lord will lack no good thing" (NLT).

Like Job, I can also say:

- Job 14:14b: "All the days of my hard service I will wait, Till my change comes" (NKJV).
- Job 42:5: "I have heard of You by the hearing of the ear, but now my eye sees You" (NKJV).

When you practice, sometimes you do not believe it will work in a game. But then that day comes where you do what you have practiced and it works, and now you are a believer and start to trust your coach even more. You will be in church hearing the word preached and taught to you and you will be wondering, *Can that really happen for me?* Well, a test will come or something will happen and then you will not just have what the pastor has said or what you have heard, but you will have experienced God for yourself and will believe and trust in Him more! You must know that while you are waiting, God is preparing you for the blessing He has for you. If you were to receive the blessing too soon, you would not be responsible or able to handle it.

## CHAPTER 5 — THE JOY IN PAIN

<u>Double Sessions</u>

After the test, it did not get any easier from there. However, it did get fun! When you are passionate about something, you cannot wait to do whatever it is you are passionate about. Some people are only game players while others are what I call complete players. And I had learned through my dad and coaches—Coach Theobald, Coach Schmidt, Coach Sartini, Coach Corrao, and Coach Graves—that practice makes perfect. See, some people have a natural ability, but you shouldn't be satisfied with just that. If someone with natural ability were to combine that with working out and practicing as if they did not have the natural ability, just think how great they could be at that sport. That is the kind of passion you should have at EVERYTHING you do. A passion to work hard, learn from those before you, put in the extra work (watch film, more time in the gym), and excel!

I had been through double sessions in high school, and even though it was hard, there were definitely some fun times even with all of the sweat, bruises, and running. I felt that I would be ready for college double sessions because Providence football had prepared me. Thankfully, I was right. You may be asking, "What are double sessions?" This is when your team has two practices in one day (morning and afternoon) for a week or two straight.

It was day one of double sessions and little did I know that we actually practiced on a field that was a mile away from our locker room. I did not realize how much I would hate that until after practices. We finally got to the field and we were all broken up into our pre-practice positions. Those who did special teams were on one side of the field, defense was on another, and then offense was at the end of the field. I remember that first day catching my first kickoff and knowing I was where I NEEDED to be.

After that we got right into practice. It was nothing like high school. After we stretched, it was go, go, go. There was no light first practice and if you did not train over the summer, it showed. I thank God for the wisdom to have discipline and to do as I was told that summer. We broke down into our individual positions and even though I did not truly want to be a receiver, that is the position I was in after talking to the coaches.

That year, double sessions were the hardest ever for me because I was in a new position with people who had played receiver all through high school. The coaches had told me they wanted my talent on the field and they were set on the running back position, so that was the reason they put me at receiver. I knew in order for me to get on the field and have a chance, I would have to work extremely hard. I not only had to try to earn a spot, but I had to beat out upperclassmen who knew the system and then freshmen who had the experience of receiving. I had to take my own advice from above and study the playbook every night.

Even though I did not want to be a receiver, I learned so much, and I believe that it made me even more dangerous as a player. There was a time where the defensive backs (DBs) would go up against the receivers during certain drills. These drills helped simulate real game situations, giving both sides the practice they needed. The one drill I remember was a tackling drill. It was for the DBs, but it also helped the receivers to work on their footwork. There would be two cones that were about 3 yards apart and that was the line of scrimmage (LOS). The DB stood about 2 yards off the LOS and the receiver stood on the LOS. The coach would say go or hike and the DB had to break down, wrap up, and tackle the receiver. The receiver's job was to make it hard for the DB and try to juke him out (put a move on him to make him miss). As a running back, we like tight spaces, so this drill helped me to enhance that skill. This was just preparation for what God would soon do.

Of course, there was a lot of trash talking by both sides and also a little underestimation. The guys I went up against thought I would be an easy target because I was not a receiver. But they quickly found out that I was a guy to be reckoned with after I juked past them and their coach made them go again. After a few practices, it ended up being me going against upperclassmen because I was really good at this particular drill. I must say, it was great making upperclassmen look bad, especially when they were standing there talking a whole bunch of trash!

The one thing that I can say is that I was honest with my ability. If I had to, I would run through the tackler, but I knew my strength and that was juking. The coaches always found a way to make practicing fun, and I loved them for it. They would put me up against the best DB and say whoever loses this one has to run, do push-ups, or something. I did not win all of them, but I won more than I lost and that was a great feeling, especially because I was in a new position.

Beyond the individual drills in double sessions, there were also the team drills. The hardest part for me as a receiver was getting used to being hit blindly. As a running back, nine out of ten times you can see where the hit is coming from and prepare yourself or juke the person out. As a receiver, sometimes you know where the DB is and can prepare for the hit. Other times you think you are wide open and out of nowhere you get punished. Every now and then you know you are going to get tackled hard and yet you still have to try to catch the ball.

So needless to say, that first week of catching the ball and taking a hit was very hard for me. There were times at practice that teammates would be disappointed because it was a catch I should have made. It was a little humbling and made me appreciate receivers more. I was used to knowing how to do my

41

position and excelling, and now I had to take a backseat and start from scratch. But there was no quitting or giving up in me because my goal was to play and I was willing to do what I needed to play.

Even though I was not doing as well as I hoped to be, I never gave up. I kept working hard, and I especially worked hard during sprints at the end of practice. I made sure that I was always working hard at the little things so that the coaches saw I had the work ethic. If they needed someone to fill in on special teams I would go. During sprints, I would always try to finish in the top five. I love a challenge, so sprints were fun for me because I always wanted to beat the upperclassmen and I wanted to show the coaches I was there to work hard.

As double sessions went on, drills got harder, the temperature got hotter, and the intensity picked up as we neared closer and closer to regular practices. I still was trying to solidify a receiver position. I improved the last week of double sessions. I started catching more balls, the offensive coach made some specific plays for me, and I was starting to think that everything might work out. The offensive coach had a reverse play for me, a fade route, and some diversion plays to use my speed to run people off. College double sessions involve a whole lot of team repetition, which I love. This gave me an opportunity to get more comfortable running plays and a chance to show what I had as well.

The joy of pain did not stop there. There was the pain of sweat, and then there was the pain of lifting. If you have ever played any type of sport, you realize that there is training that goes along with that sport so that your body can handle the punishment or work that comes with it. I have heard people who play sports say that they hate lifting. Or I have seen people who take lifting and training for granted and do not work hard at it. These are the people who want a quick fix and want all the glory without the hard work.

In order to be a great gymnast, you have to have the muscles to jump and to pull yourself up. To be a great football player, you have to be able to take a few hits. To be a great runner, you have to not only have endurance, but your muscles must be strong enough to do the event you are great at. What do all of these things have in common? No matter what sport you are in, you must train your body to handle the physical aspects of that sport. My Lord, that was a revelation for me on my spiritual walk!

I think about how I turned out as a football player and what I would have been had I not worked as hard as I did to become physically ready. I mentioned earlier in this book that I had decided to stop playing basketball so I could get in the weight room and get bigger. I knew that I was not going to grow anymore so there was no need to focus on that. I had to focus on what I knew I could control, which was to get faster and stronger. I have said it before and I will say it again, my father and mother were and still are my biggest fans. I had a mission, they supported that mission, and they made sure I had everything I needed to complete that mission.

In college, my mission did not change one bit. I knew I was not the typical size for a receiver or a running back, but that just made me more determined to work hard and get better every day. The great thing about college was that if you had the passion and burning desire (that is what we said all the time at Providence) to give it 110%, you had all the resources you needed to get it done. You cannot make someone passionate about something; that has to come from within them. However, you can make someone better and all it takes is a plan, goals, and discipline. I had the speed as a youngster and the talent was there, but I knew from the lessons my father taught me and seeing those who were truly great in sports (Jerry Rice and Michael Jordan, to name a few) that I had to continue to get better and not get complacent.

43

So, taking those goals into account, I worked hard in the weight room while I was at Butler. We had a personal trainer who had a regimen that we had to follow each week. I tell you now, college lifting was no playing around. During double sessions, you hit the weights pretty hard. Not once did I ever leave that weight room without my shirt drenched. Sometimes our trainer would come up with workout activities at the end of the workout that pushed me to the max.

For instance, after we finished lifting for an hour, he would have a tire set up in the weight room. This was not a regular tire that goes on a car. I am talking about a tire that goes on a semi. We had to flip the tire from one end of the weight room all the way to the other end and the weight room was not small. By the time you finished lifting and completing the special activities he prepared at the end of workouts, your muscles were sore. But after a few months of this, I was seeing the joy in pain. I could see and feel the difference in my body. My hard work made me more effective as a player and able to handle those hits I was talking about earlier.

One of the most important things I had to do as a player was replenish. From running, lifting, and practices, I had to make sure that I always drank a lot of water and Gatorade to keep myself hydrated. I was working so hard and pouring out so much sweat that I had to make sure I replenished the inside! It is so important that I was taken care of on the inside because if you do not drink enough of the RIGHT liquids it will have an effect on your physical body. It is also important that you understand the power of three. You cannot just get it right in one area, but it must be all three areas: practice, lifting, eating/drinking. I can take that a step further and say body, mind, and soul. I could even go at the highest level of the big three (not talking about the Golden State Warriors) and say the Father, Son, and Holy Spirit! It is important to develop and know all three to be COMPLETE!

The one thing you can never truly do is fake yourself out. You can try to say you are okay, but inside you really know you are not. You can try to do a lot on the outside to be the best, but know on the inside there are some voids that need to be filled. When you really work hard and do your best even when you do not feel like it all the time, you feel joy on the inside because you have done all you can. That is why there can be joy in pain. The joy comes from the inside knowing that you left it on the field! Even when the coach yells at you to do better, you take that and apply it because you realize you can still learn and get better. No one is perfect, but our coaches want us to be the best we can be.

Not only that, but our coaches sometimes see things in us that we do not see or have not even thought about. That is why we must love coaches because they push us beyond what we can fathom. You may have had a coach that was not the best, but God is always a loving coach. It is for this reason you will love Coach God. He wants you to succeed, do your best, and because of Jesus, God sees who you really are. Work hard, set goals, have discipline, and do what you have the passion to do! You may not be the biggest, the strongest, or the smartest, but if you have a passion for something, work hard, and think about the joy you will gain, it will all add up to victory in the end!

## Victory Testimony:
One Door Closes, Another Opens

I'll never forget what Mr. Campbell said to me that day. He sounded so confident. First day of senior year was like every other first day of school. Everyone looked good and smelled good. Every senior was excited to start their last first day of high school. Every day before class started, I usually went to my counselor's office. I walked in and it looked like Mrs. Sowder was renovating her office. She did not have her soft country radio playing, and the smell of her room was absent of flowers and sweet stuff; it smelled like nothing. The room looked like a man's office: no posters, no music, and no girly smell. I soon realized she left to go counsel at a new high school. My heart sank when the head secretary told me she was not coming back and that Mr. Campbell took her position as the new guidance counselor. I thought to myself, *Who am I supposed to talk to?* I was not going to talk to a man about my problems. Little did I know God had a different plan for me. Later in first semester, Mr. Campbell called me down to do the normal check-up on grades. Before I even realized it, my eyes were watering, and I started to vent. After that day, I went to his office for everything. Mr. Campbell had such an impact on me my senior year. He helped me grow spiritually, mentally, and emotionally.

I'll never forget the words Mr. Campbell said to me that day. He was so confident in what the Lord had said to him. Mr. Campbell said, "Lauren, I bet you forgive your mom. I bet she gets sober by the time you leave for college and that you will have a relationship with her." I just sat there and thought my mom would never sober up, let alone have a healthy relationship with me. I just laughed at Mr. Campbell's ridiculous idea.

My mom was not the ideal type of mother. She once was this strong independent woman who taught her daughters morals and values. I used to envy her. I needed Mr. Campbell more than ever my senior year of high school. My mom and I did not have the best relationship. It started in middle school and that's when my mom took a turn for the worst. She was working all the time, partying all the time, and sleeping around all the time. It just was not the mother I once knew. She became very depressed, bitter, and angry. She constantly chose drugs, alcohol, and men over me. She would have rather taken that next drink than watch one of my ball games or take me out shopping. I later found out my senior year that my mom was diagnosed with manic bipolar disorder. Drinking and not taking her medicine regularly did not help the cause.

Mr. Campbell knew all of this and still told me everything was going to be okay. "You just have to have a little bit of faith," he said. I did not understand at the time what he meant. He started to read me scriptures every day and ask me to come to prayer group every morning before school. I was learning about Christianity a lot more than I ever did when I was a kid. I guess I took it more seriously because I was older, and I could understand it more. God did not mean much to me at the time. I thought I could handle everything on my own. I did not really get the whole concept. Mr. Campbell invited me to his church and, at the time, I felt obligated to go. There was something in my gut that said I needed to go. After attending I decided that day that Canaan Christian Church was my new home. Mr. Campbell's church changed my whole view on Christ. I went to church every Wednesday and every Sunday before I left for college. Every day I could see myself molding into a Christian. Canaan opened their arms to me as if I was their own. The church showed me a new way of life that I would have not gotten without them. Mr. Campbell gave me the push and the motivation to start a strong, serious relationship with my higher power.

Gradually, during the time I was becoming a Christian, there were things changing all around me: people, places, and even me. I saw changes in my mom, dad, and even my sister that I never thought I would have seen. I saw my prayers being answered, and I felt like a better person inside and out. I started to realize what being a Christian was all about. I knew I needed to forgive, not for my mom's sake, but for my own. Carrying the burden around only weighed me down, not my mom.

I knew it was time to forgive my mom after I went to my last bible study at Canaan. The topic of the day at bible study was forgiveness. Bible study always found a way to make things clear as day to me. I knew if God forgives us for sinning, why keep holding on to my burden? I had this sense of clarity like God was speaking to me. I never thought I would have the strength or courage to tell my mom how I really felt about her. I rehearsed so many times in Mr. Campbell's office of how I was going to approach my mom. It was like practicing an acting scene. I finally told my mom that I forgave her. It kind of just came out in the car on our way to a family outing. It happened so fast I really did not know what I was even saying. It was a powerful moment. I felt like all the heavy burden was lifted off my shoulders, like I was set free. Like I could go to college now and be okay with leaving my family.

A week before I left for college, my mom and I rebuilt our relationship, and she stopped using. It felt like déjà vu all over again. To actually think Mr. Campbell was right was hard to take in. I never thought in a million years my mom and I would have a healthy relationship and she would be sober at the same time. I never thought I would actually forgive her either. The last Sunday I was in town I asked my mom to go to church with me. She actually said yes. My mom accepted Jesus Christ in her life that day and I could not believe it when my mom walked down to the altar. I was so proud of my mom that day. That week was probably the best week I ever spent with my mom. We finally put all the chaos aside and truly spent quality time together. I would take that seven days over any bad day. Growing as a Christian was hard and still is tough sometimes. It is amazing what God has in store for us. I've witnessed things and heard things that I never thought I would if I had not found God. I was struggling and Mr. Campbell saved me from all the chaos around. I started to look more into the positive. It was finally nice to have someone I could always count on: God. I can only thank Mr. Campbell for giving me the guidance he gave me. He showed me the path of God's righteousness: the way, the truth, and the life. At the end of the day, I was glad Mrs.

Sowder left because if she had not, I would have never stepped into Mr. Campbell's office that day. When one door closes, another one always opens.
—Lauren Camm

## REFLECTION

Now that you have been tested between the lines of life, it is time to put in the hard work. Ask yourself, "Do I need to put in more time? Do I need to take bigger steps? Am I still on the right path to reach my goal or do I need to make an adjustment?"

## FAITH WALK

➢ Hebrews 12:1-2: "Therefore, since we are surrounded by such a huge crowd of witnesses to the life of faith, let us strip off every weight that slows us down, especially the sin that so easily trips us up. And let us run with endurance the race God has set before us. We do this by keeping our eyes on Jesus, the champion who initiates and perfects our faith. Because of the joy awaiting him, he endured the cross, disregarding its shame. Now he is seated in the place of honor beside God's throne" (NLT).

All the preparation of double sessions, lifting weights, memorizing plays, meetings with your position coach, and practicing is for a greater purpose. It seems hard, and the process seems long, but when the game comes, it is all worth it. If it had not been for all the preparation, you would not be ready for the game. This is also true for the Christian life. You are running a race for Christ and in order to win this race you must be prepared and go through the processes of life.

The first thing you must understand is that there are some people who have already won the race. When you read the Bible, it tells of people like us who **trusted** and **believed** in God, and He supernaturally brought them through whatever they were facing. In Hebrews chapter 11, the Bible names some of these

49

people of faith. So know that if God can do it for them, He can and will do it for you. I hear you saying, "Well you do not know my situation or understand what I have been through." You are absolutely right! However, there is a God who knows about your situation and if you will lean on Him and trust Him, He WILL work it out. Yes, I hear you saying, "God did it then, but He won't do it for me now." Well I am here, as a witness, to tell you that He WILL do it and CONTINUES to do it TODAY!

➢ Hebrews 13:8: "Jesus Christ *is* the same yesterday, today, and forever" (NKJV).

The next thing you must do is set aside every weight and sin that keeps you from running the race properly. This race you are running should give God glory. Just as you want to make your coach proud by doing what he says and expects of you, you should want to do the same and more for God. Let's do a mini-evaluation:

1) Do you obey your parents? Exodus 20:12 says, "Honor your father and mother. Then you will live a long, full life in the land the Lord your God is giving you" (NLT). Also, look at Matthew 19:19 in NKJV.

2) Are you cursing? Ephesians 4:29 says, "Don't use foul or abusive language. Let everything you say be good and helpful, so that your words will be an encouragement to those who hear them" (NLT). Titus 3:2 says, "They must not slander anyone and must avoid quarreling. Instead, they should be gentle and show true humility to everyone" (NLT).

3) Are you doing sexual acts (not just sex)? 1 Corinthians 6:18-20 says, "Run from sexual sin! No other sin so clearly affects the body as this one does. For sexual immorality is a sin against your own body. Don't you realize that your body is the temple of the Holy Spirit, who lives in you and was given to you by God? You do not belong to yourself, for God bought you with a high price. So you must honor God with your body" (NLT).

4) Do you read your Bible? Joshua 1:8 says, "This Book of the Law shall not depart out of your mouth, but you shall read [and meditate on] it day and night, so that you may be careful to do [everything] in accordance with all that is written in it; for then you shall make your way prosperous, and then you will be successful" (AMP).

5) Do you smoke cigarettes, any other substance, and/or take pills? 1 Corinthians 3:16-17 says, "You realize, don't you, that you are the temple of God, and God himself is present in you? No one will get by with vandalizing God's temple, you can be sure of that. God's temple is sacred—and you, remember, *are* the temple" (MSG).

6) Do you get drunk? (It is okay to socially drink, meaning to drink occasionally and not get drunk or tipsy.) Ephesians 5:15-21 says, "So be careful how you live. Don't live like fools, but like those who are wise. Make the most of every opportunity in these evil days. Don't act thoughtlessly, but understand what the Lord wants you to do. Don't be drunk with wine, because that will ruin your life. Instead, be filled with the Holy Spirit, singing psalms and hymns and spiritual songs among yourselves, and making music to the Lord in your hearts. And give thanks for everything to God the Father in the name of our Lord Jesus Christ. And further, submit to one another out of reverence for Christ" (NLT). You can also read 1 Corinthians 6:9-10 (NLT), Galatians 5:19-21 (NLT), and 1 Peter 4:1-3 (NIV).

7) Do you lie and gossip? Proverbs 8:6-8 says, "Listen, for I will speak of excellent things, And from the opening of my lips *will come* right things; For my mouth will speak truth; Wickedness *is* an abomination to my lips. All the words of my mouth *are* with righteousness; Nothing crooked or perverse *is* in them" (NKJV). Proverbs 15:7 (NLT) later continues with, "The lips of the wise give good advice; the heart of a fool has none to give" and "A gossip goes around telling secrets, so don't hang around with chatterers" (Proverbs 20:19, NLT).

I could go on with this list, but the point here is that you have to change your thinking so that you can change your actions and then the way you live.

> Romans 12:2: "Don't copy the behavior and customs of this world, but let God transform you into a new person by changing the way you think. Then you will learn to know God's will for you, which is good and pleasing and perfect" (NLT).

The life you live should give God glory. You should help one another, encouraging instead of gossiping and talking about others. Be thankful instead of being envious or jealous of what others have, and pray instead of hoping for good luck, reading horoscopes, or leaving it to chance. Romans 12:9-18 (NLT) offers great guidance in this area. I can hear you right now saying, "Well that kind of life does not sound fun." You could not be further from the truth.

You have been gradually seduced by the devil to think that drinking, partying, clubbing, sex, drugs, fooling around, being popular, being rich, etc. is what life is about. I thought these were vital at one point, too. The devil has even made you think that you are supposed to do these things while you are young and then change after the age of 40 or so. Again, he wants you to keep chasing fame, fortune, and being promiscuous so that you will not have a relationship with God, a fulfilled life, and will not be able to bless others as God has purposed. But if you will let God order your steps NOW, TODAY, then the new, complete you will see that life with God is not only fun, but it is a blessing.

> Proverbs 8:34-35: "Blessed is the man who listens to me, Watching daily at my gates, Waiting at the posts of my doors. For whoever finds me finds life, And obtains favor from the Lord" (NKJV).

I have not always been in such a stable, faithful place as I am now, but I thank God that He showed me a new lifestyle.

When you get the right friends around you who know and believe in God, you will have a blast. Going out will be different than before because you will have a different mindset and you will be with those who have the right mindset about God. You can watch movies, skate, bowl, and have a godly party at your house with music and dancing. This does not have to be godly music, but it should not be degrading. Have a fellowship where you talk about what is going on and encourage each other with the Word of God. As you get older, you may go out every now and then for an occasion, but it is not every weekend and you represent yourself as a Christian. The truth is, there is no set age for godly living because the closer you walk with Christ, He will show you where you do not need to be or go.

Lastly, there will be some pain while running the race. This pain, even though at first you may not see it, will turn to joy. Jesus died on the cross because He knew it was for a greater good. His death and resurrection did not only open the door for eternal life and forgiveness of sins for you, but Jesus knew that He would be raised and would sit down at the right hand of the Father. You must realize that you are an extension of the work of Christ in someone's life today. You are saved (or hopefully will read this, become saved, and join a church) and the Holy Spirit lives inside of you. The same power that raised Jesus up from the grave is inside of you.

> ➢ Romans 8:11: "The Spirit of God, who raised Jesus from the dead, lives in you. And just as God raised Christ Jesus from the dead, he will give life to your mortal bodies by this same Spirit living within you" (NLT).

You are to continue the work of Jesus until you die and then one day meet Him face to face. Is this easy to do when there are people talking about you, trying to take what you have, and do not believe what you believe? NO! But if you endure through the race to completion, not only will God bless you, but He will be with you the whole time.

➢ Matthew 28:20: "Teach these new disciples to obey all the commands I have given you. And be sure of this: I am with you always, even to the end of the age" (NLT).

➢ Hebrews 13:5-6: "Don't love money; be satisfied with what you have. For God has said, 'I will never fail you. I will never abandon you.' So we can say with confidence, 'The Lord is my helper, so I will have no fear. What can mere people do to me?'" (NLT).

➢ Galatians 6:7-10: "Don't be misled—you cannot mock the justice of God. You will always harvest what you plant. Those who live only to satisfy their own sinful nature will harvest decay and death from that sinful nature. But those who live to please the Spirit will harvest everlasting life from the Spirit. So let's not get tired of doing what is good. At just the right time we will reap a harvest of blessing if we don't give up.
Therefore, whenever we have the opportunity, we should do good to everyone—especially to those in the family of faith" (NLT).

If you do well, you will reap a great harvest. Just remember that your timing may not be God's. Even when you think He is late, He is always right on time! My favorite scripture says it best: "The joy of the Lord is your strength" (Nehemiah 8:10b, NKJV). Forget the past and rejoice that your future will be better because you are going to lean on the Lord to direct your path rather than your own wisdom.

➢ Proverbs 3:5-6: "Trust in *and* rely confidently on the Lord with all your heart and do not rely on your own insight *or* understanding. In all your ways know *and* acknowledge *and* recognize Him, and He will make your paths straight *and* smooth [removing obstacles that block your way]" (AMP).

No matter what sport you play, you must have the right equipment. I thank God that the worst injury I sustained while playing football was a wrist injury and a few sprained ankles.

Why? I had the proper pads on to protect me. Well, during your Christian race you better be girded up with the armor of God.

> Ephesians 6:10-18: "A final word: Be strong in the Lord and in his mighty power. Put on all of God's armor so that you will be able to stand firm against all strategies of the devil. For we are not fighting against flesh-and-blood enemies, but against evil rulers and authorities of the unseen world, against mighty powers in this dark world, and against evil spirits in the heavenly places. Therefore, put on every piece of God's armor so you will be able to resist the enemy in the time of evil. Then after the battle you will still be standing firm. Stand your ground, putting on the belt of truth and the body armor of God's righteousness. For shoes, put on the peace that comes from the Good News so that you will be fully prepared. In addition to all of these, hold up the shield of faith to stop the fiery arrows of the devil. Put on salvation as your helmet, and take the sword of the Spirit, which is the word of God. Pray in the Spirit at all times and on every occasion. Stay alert and be persistent in your prayers for all believers everywhere" (NLT).

When you are equipped with the right armor, the devil can try to come against you but it won't work because you are ready. Satan will try to throw depression at you, but you have your helmet of salvation. The enemy will try to lead you down a wrong path, but you have on your shoes of peace. The devil will try to tempt you with old habits, but you have the sword of the spirit, which is the Word of God, to fight back. The enemy will try to take you out and kill you but you have the breast plate of righteousness (see John 10:10 NKJV). Finally, the devil will throw some darts of past relationships, past abuse, doubt, and fears, but you have the shield of faith to block them and any other temptation (see 1 Corinthians 10:13, NKJV).

Let us look at a quick example of how important it is to have your own equipment. In 1 Samuel 17:34-39, we see where

Saul tries to put his armor on David before he goes up against Goliath, the Philistine. Verse 39 says, "David fastened his sword to his armor and tried to walk, for he had not tested *them*. And David said to Saul, 'I cannot walk with these, for I have not tested *them*.' So David took them off" (NKJV). When you play a sport, you have practiced with the same equipment for days and days before game day. The purpose of wearing the equipment before game day is so that you know how to move in it. David realized that if he had worn Saul's equipment, he would not have been able to move and might have lost the battle with Goliath. (He won by using a slingshot and one smooth stone that hit Goliath in his forehead.) As a Christian, it is important for you to trust and rely on the armor of God and His word. And to take it a step further, it is important that you have the right players with you who can help you pray your way to victory.

Remember that this race is not going to be easy nor without difficulties. This race will have tests, bumps in the road, and bad weather. God will be with you and will provide for you what you need. Be confident that God's tests are to develop you into what He knows you can be and the devil's attempts to destroy you are so that you do not become what God knows you can be (see Romans 5:3-5 and James 1:2-4 in NLT).

- ➢ 1 John 4:4: "Little children (believers, dear ones), you are of God *and* you belong to Him and have [already] overcome them [the agents of the antichrist]; because He Who lives in you is greater than he (Satan) who is in the world [of sinful mankind]" (AMP).
- ➢ Genesis 39:21-23: "But the LORD was with Joseph in the prison and showed him his faithful love. And the LORD made Joseph a favorite with the prison warden. Before long, the warden put Joseph in charge of all the other prisoners and over everything that happened in the prison. The warden had no more worries, because

Joseph took care of everything. The LORD was with
him and caused everything he did to succeed" (NLT).
Joseph was lied to and put in prison, yet God was with him and
caused him to succeed.  God will do the same for you in your
situation and allow people to bless you and cause you to succeed.

## Chapter 6 – Responsible Routine

In life, we tend to get into routines, but if I were to look at your routines could you say they are responsible? I could have just as easily named this chapter "Temptation." For those first two weeks, school was simple: no class, not many people on campus, and I knew what was coming each day. That all would change soon. Soon there would be around 4,500 students on campus, class with homework and assignments, girls, parties, and more football. I was about to get a taste of what being a college athlete was really about.

Let me start at move-in day and welcome week. It was the first day of move-in for the entire campus. To be honest, I don't know if I was excited or upset because it was nice having the whole dorm to ourselves and we (the sports teams that were there) had all gotten close. But regardless of how I felt, the students started rolling in. I had practice that morning so when I got done and came back to the dorms, the halls were full of students, parents, friends, siblings, and helpers moving students in. Since I was in a co-ed dorm, I believe my perception and feelings quickly changed after I saw some of the girls who would be staying in my dorm. This was the one day that all the entrances to the girls' floor were open. So a few of the football players, including me, did some scouting of our own to see what we would be dealing with for the year. We did actually help out a little, too.

I am sure some students felt intimidated or nervous just as I did when I first walked in to meet the football team, because a lot of us were already hanging out in groups of four or more because we had been there for two weeks. I remember meeting my roommates who were beside me and across the hall. I also met more people from the time I stepped on campus till I graduated; I was always meeting people. There are so many opportunities to meet and build relationships with students and faculty that you should have enough contacts by the time you graduate to help you get your foot in the door for a job or in touch with someone who can help you.

During the first few days of move-in, the school had what they called "Welcome Week." Butler had a beautiful lawn that went through the middle of the campus, which was called "The Mall." This is where Welcome Week was held. They had tents set up with food. They had different programs set up on the sidewalk that you could sign up for, and they had games to help you get to know others. I got to participate in most of these activities.

The other thing I liked about Welcome Week is that we worked in groups. They chose our groups, which was good because it put the athletes in different groups, allowing me to meet more people. Sometimes we have a tendency to stay with what is comfortable rather than to step out and have faith to try something new. Had I stayed with my friends on the football team, it may have been a pattern that I would have remained in for a while. But because I was taken out of my comfort zone, I made new friends and had fun doing it. So, what I thought would be boring and lame turned out to be fun and beneficial. You never know how much you can learn until you take a step of faith!

Once Welcome Week was over and everyone was moved in, it meant it was time to start my college education. I had been at college for a few weeks and it seemed like the life: play football, hang out, and no school. But the first day of classes was upon us and I had my schedule, knew where I was going, and had all my books. One extra piece of advice at this point: make sure that you get along with your academic advisor. Your advisor will help guide you and keep you on track to graduate. If you do not see eye to eye with this person, then get a new one. If you feel your advisor is not helpful or too busy, get a new one.

The worst part about being an athlete is that you have to start your day with the earliest classes possible. For football, we started practice around 3:30PM, which meant we had to be done with classes by 2:30PM. So I started my day at 8AM every morning. You also had to get your two or three days of lifting in during the week. So if you had a break between classes you could not relax. You had to use that time to go lift. Then you had to fit in lunch, dinner, and homework.

I hear you saying, "It must be easier in the off-season." And the response to that is NO! In the off-season, there was a point where we met at 6AM to complete team workouts because it is hard to get the whole team together. Then we still had to fit workouts in our schedules four times a week and meet with position coaches, and before we knew it, it was time for spring football.

Finally, we had the parties, hanging out in friends' rooms, the girls, and the city life of Indianapolis, IN. Just in the city alone, there is plenty to do: movie theater, mall, museum, zoo, baseball games, basketball games, football games, and all sorts of special events. On campus, there were house parties, fraternity parties, and dorm room parties. Then, throw girls into the mix and trying to figure out which one was cool, which one liked me, and who I could hang out with or date.

With all that you may have going on, plus athletics and your education—which is why I was there—how do you stay focused and responsible? It's a great question. The first thing is, you have to be responsible before you get into college. You have to have good habits that carry over from high school.

One thing my parents always stressed was that I had to have my homework done before I could go anywhere or do anything. My parents always made sure that I was organized, had enough folders to separate my subjects, and had a planner to write down due dates for assignments and projects. However, whether you go to school at home or you go away to school, you have to want to succeed and that comes from within. Parents can provide help, and mine did, but you still have to apply the tools they have given you in order to be successful.

After my first week of classes, I had all of my syllabuses and knew what I had to do for the whole year. Even with as much discipline as I have, it was tough at times in the off-season to do my homework right away. Starting my day at 8AM every day felt like a half day of school. Some days I had three or four classes and other days I had only one class. So knowing that I had only so much time, it got tough. It also was tough because I wanted to hang out with the new friends I had just met, watch movies in their room, play pool downstairs in the activity room, and play music and dance. As you recall, earlier I said that I named my room "Club Sweetness," so this was a distraction I added to myself. I would leave my door open and play music while studying and that always brought people in. Yes, it was fun, but it made for some long nights because one way or another, I had to finish that work.

As the days passed, I realized that the dorm was a tough place to study. You can hear everything that goes on in the building. People were always knocking at my door to see if I was there and it is also noisy. I finally had to give in and start using the library. This is where being responsible comes into play. You have to evaluate what you are doing and be honest with yourself. I knew that what I was doing was not working. After evaluating myself, I then had to come up with a routine. There were some variables in play that I knew were not going to change. Those variables were football practice, classes, lifting time, and eating. So I had to come up with times and places to study and complete my homework and papers.

If you notice, I did not mention hanging out. There was not much of that during the season, except on Saturday after the games (if they were at home) and Sundays. As an athlete, you will have a curfew. You have to be rested so you can perform and give your body the rest it needs to recover and build at the same time. I hung out with friends usually during lunch and during dinner. You have to be tight with the players on your team because that is who you see most of the time. I was not in a fraternity, but I considered my football teammates my fraternity brothers.

Now I will be honest and say that there were a couple fraternity parties that I went to the night before a game as a freshman. However, I did not drink and I did not stay out late. I tell you this so you realize that there are all kinds of temptations that will try to pull you this way and that way and deter you from your goals. I could have gotten busted being out for a few hours of dancing and fun and forfeited my position I had earned on the team. As I kept evaluating my decisions, I had to ask myself, as should you, "IS IT WORTH IT?" Are the few seconds of fun, the few seconds of talking to that girl, the few seconds of one exciting night, worth something that could determine your future and possibly your life? And for me, the answer was NO!

I stopped going out before games and realized that I had to be responsible and trustworthy with what I had been entrusted with. At some point, you have to stop playing around and get serious about your passion! I thank God it only took part of my freshman year to realize that what I was doing was dumb and could have not only hurt me, but also my teammates who depended on me being able to do my part at the game. Part of my responsibility was being rested and mentally and physically ready.

One of the biggest and most important things that I had to fit into my routine was church. My church home is Canaan Christian Church in Louisville, KY, where my pastor is Dr. Walter Malone Jr. It is amazing looking back at how God worked things out. Two years in a row, our church invited a pastor from Indianapolis to preach at our church conference. At the time, I thought nothing of it because I did not know where I would be going to school. But the thing about God is, where He leads you He will provide. So once I knew I was going to Butler, I asked my pastor about Jeffrey Johnson, who was the pastor who preached at our conference two years in a row. My pastor definitely gave his approval.

Once I got to Indianapolis, I got in contact with my cousin who also attended his church. I started to attend on Sundays. I eventually joined Eastern Star Church under "watch care." I was still a member at Canaan, but I now also sat under the spiritual covering of Pastor Johnson while I was at school. For me, church was not an option when I was growing up because my parents made me go, which should be the case for youth TODAY as well.

However, when I was at college, it was a choice. I had the choice of doing what I knew was right. I had the choice of going so that I could receive a word from God that would enhance my life and bless me. I also had a choice to sleep in and forget about God for four years after all he had done for me and was doing for me. I chose to wake up and go to church regardless of being hurt or tired.

I needed balance and the only way I would have balance was to keep God first. Too many times we don't take God everywhere we go. We go on vacation and we leave Him at home. We hang out with certain friends and we leave Him at home. We listen to Christian music, yet let someone get in the car who does not and we turn the station. We go off to college and forget about church until we visit home. If we are to grow in Christ and if we are to hear from God, we must continue to seek him every day and everywhere we go. I know that for me, while I was at college, God helped me through circumstances and delivered me from many problems.

To be a little transparent, I mentioned earlier about the girls and the temptations. If I am being honest, I loved to flirt with the girls and mess around, but I really was not the guy who wanted to have sex. Did I fall short and do it a few times? Yes. However, it was my own fault. With sincerity, I would tell girls that I was talking to or messing around with that I did not want to have sex, and that we were just going to mess around. My problem, which I figured out around my junior year in college, was that I was setting myself up with these temptations and trusting that these girls were on the same page as I was. The Lord showed me that I was putting myself into the temptation and I was failing because I was putting my trust in girls, expecting them to honor my wishes. The Lord showed me that I should have been more focused on honoring Him.

But when you are trying to walk in God's light, the enemy will not leave you alone that easily. So as God showed me this, I started to ease away from putting myself in tempting situations. Then I turned to pornography. The enemy had me believing that if I did this, at least I was not having sex and I was not hurting anyone. But when God has his hands on you, when you are going to church and being fed the word of God, and when you are praying and seeking him on a daily basis, God has a way of opening your eyes so that you can see the truth. Then you can be set free. God showed me that pornography was nothing but a false love. He showed me that pornography was not how sex should be, and it was perverting my mind and my image of love.

I encourage you today, if you are reading this book, find a church home. Find some students or friends that you can go to church and talk about God with, and live it in your life. Do not be ashamed to be a Christian. I can tell you from experience that if you serve Him wholeheartedly, in due time He will open the windows of heaven and pour blessings on you! Choose today to evaluate your routine and ask yourself, "Am I being responsible with the power that has been entrusted to me?"

## Victory Testimony:

Justin came into my life in the seventh grade. Middle school is a very critical time in an adolescent's life. I believe it's when you start to decide what path you are going to take. And at that time, I wasn't choosing a very good one. I was making poor choices and hanging around the wrong crowd. I had a bad attitude and treated people poorly. That's when Justin became my mentor. He helped steer me in the right direction. He would take me to lunch and do different activities with me. He was basically like my big brother. He was such a positive role model and he helped me strive to be a better person. He taught me how to be a positive influence to the people around me. And as time progressed, I stopped getting in trouble and I began to hang around people who lifted me up instead of dragging me down. I finished my middle school and high school career without getting in any trouble. After high school, I got my Commercial Driver's License and became a truck driver at Sodrel Truck Lines. I now have two beautiful children, Ava and Asher, and beautiful girlfriend. If it weren't for Justin, I have no doubt that I wouldn't be the successful man that I am today. Justin changed my life and I am forever grateful for him.

—Ray Hicks

## REFLECTION

Everyone wants to have control, but with control comes accountability. Do you feel in control of the steps you are taking? Do you feel that you are making responsible choices? Do you have an accountability partner that can help you on your journey?

## FAITH WALK

Responsible means to be trustworthy or able to choose for oneself between right and wrong. Routine is a regular course of procedure, a habit. You have to ask yourself, "Is what I am choosing on a regular or ordinary basis right or wrong?" If you can take a deep look at yourself and your bad habits, God is going to sift somethings and shift you. A sifter is a cooking utensil that separates the good from the bad. For example, when you have been dipping chicken in the flour and it gets clumpy, you then pour the flour into the sifter and the flour will go through the net while the bad flour that is clumpy will stay on the net so you can discard it. He is going to shift you because as you evaluate yourself based on the word of God, you will change your thinking from the world's ways to God's way. Therefore, a shift in position. There truly is only one way.

➢ John 14:6: "Jesus told him, 'I am the way, the truth, and the life. No one can come to the Father except through me'" (NLT).

When you shift, He will sift. When you start to focus on God and his plan for your life, He will take the bad habits out of you and the good deposits will start to come out. This is why it is wrong to think that you have to get it right first before coming to church. The church is your spiritual hospital and will help the shift take place.

➢ Mark 2:16-17: "And when the scribes and Pharisees saw Him eating with the tax collectors and sinners, they said to His disciples, 'How *is it* that He eats and drinks with tax collectors and sinners?' When Jesus heard *it*, He said to them, 'Those who are well have no need of a physician, but those who are sick. I did not come to call the righteous, but sinners, to repentance'" (NKJV).

The great news is you were created in His image and likeness, so it has always been there. Now that you are saved—brought back into a right relationship with God—and His Spirit lives in you, you can see it. One way you can shift is by this scripture:

> Galatians 5:22-23: "But the fruit of the Spirit is love, joy, peace, longsuffering, kindness, goodness, faithfulness, gentleness, self-control. Against such there is no law" (NKJV).

When it says there is no law, it means if you exhibit these qualities there is no law because you fulfill it by showing these Christ-like qualities. We thank Jesus that He left us the Holy Spirit, who has written the laws on our hearts and minds to teach and comfort us through our journey.

In the last discussion, I asked you a few questions, but in this section I am going to dive in a little deeper. I pray now that as you are reading this, you will be open to let God change your thinking, mold your heart, and transform your actions to align with His will. Please read Romans 12 in NLT for guidance. Let's look in the Bible and see what is not a responsible routine. Some of these will look really familiar to you.

> 1 Corinthians 6:9-11: "Don't you realize that those who do wrong will not inherit the Kingdom of God? Don't fool yourselves. Those who indulge in sexual sin, or who worship idols, or commit adultery, or are male prostitutes, or practice homosexuality, or are thieves, or greedy people, or drunkards, or are abusive, or cheat people—none of these will inherit the Kingdom of God. Some of you were once like that. But you were cleansed; you were made holy; you were made right with God by calling on the name of the Lord Jesus Christ and by the Spirit of our God" (NLT).

> Galatians 5:19-21: "When you follow the desires of your sinful nature, the results are very clear: sexual immorality, impurity, lustful pleasures, idolatry, sorcery, hostility, quarreling, jealousy, outbursts of anger, selfish ambition, dissension, division, envy, drunkenness, wild parties [orgies], and other sins like these. Let me tell you again, as I have before, that anyone living that sort of life will not inherit the Kingdom of God" (NLT).

➤ Ephesians 5:3-5: "But among you there must not be even a hint of sexual immorality, or of any kind of impurity, or of greed, because these are improper for God's holy people. Nor should there be obscenity, foolish talk or coarse joking, which are out of place, but rather thanksgiving. For of this you can be sure: No immoral, impure or greedy person—such a person is an idolater—has any inheritance in the kingdom of Christ and of God" (NIV).

If you are fornicating (having sex before marriage), coarse joking (doing harsh pranks or making dirty, sexual jokes), foolish talking, being hateful, selfish, or envious, having drunken parties, or are involved in homosexuality/lesbianism, then you need to change your routine. Genesis 2 tells us that the man is to leave mother and father and be joined to his wife. However, the enemy always tries to pervert what God has done. Let me also say that regardless, you are to love people—whatever the sin—and not judge, and instead help them understand the word of God.

Part of this routine may be because of the atmosphere you put yourself in and the people you *allow* to come into your life. It is very true when people say, "You take on the characteristics of the people you hang with." You may want to evaluate the characteristics of those you are hanging with, and if they do not align with what God is looking for, you have to cut them out of your life. It is like a weed. If that weed is not removed, it will choke the good seeds that have grown. Likewise, if you do not remove the people that God did not plant in your life, they will choke some of the good seeds that have been planted in you. Let God prune and cut so you may bear greater fruit (read John 15:1-2 in NLT for reference).

Secondly, you have to watch where you go. Some places will have you doing some things you should not be doing, but you do it because of the habits that are in you. You also have to watch where you go because the atmosphere is evil and may overpower *your* will to do right. To make this plain, think about climate. Climate is determined by the average condition of the weather at a place usually over a period of years as exhibited by temperature, wind velocity, and precipitation. If you were to move to San Diego, California, you probably know that the atmosphere is good because on average the climate is 75 degrees. You have the choice to consistently put the right people around you, watch where you go, be careful of what you watch on TV and at the movies, watch what you listen to, and even watch what you eat. Make the choice today to search for the climate that works for you so that your atmosphere will be pleasing to God.

Above I mentioned good seeds. Now let's look at a responsible routine pleasing to God.

- ➢ Galatians 5:16-18: "So I say, let the Holy Spirit guide your lives. Then you won't be doing what your sinful nature craves. The sinful nature wants to do evil, which is just the opposite of what the Spirit wants. And the Spirit gives us desires that are the opposite of what the sinful nature desires. These two forces are constantly fighting each other, so you are not free to carry out your good intentions. But when you are directed by the Spirit, you are not under obligation to the law of Moses" (NLT).
- ➢ Galatians 5:24-26: "Those who belong to Christ Jesus have nailed the passions and desires of their sinful nature to his cross and crucified them there. Since we are living by the Spirit, let us follow the Spirit's leading in every part of our lives. Let us not become conceited, or provoke one another, or be jealous of one another" (NLT).
- ➢ Matthew 22:37-40: "Jesus replied, 'You must love the Lord your God with all your heart, all your soul, and all your mind.' This is the first and greatest

commandment. A second is equally important: 'Love your neighbor as yourself.' The entire law and all the demands of the prophets are based on these two commandments" (NLT).

> John 13:34: "A new commandment I give to you, that you love one another; as I have loved you, that you also love one another" (NKJV).

I added this because the word "new" here does not mean different, but instead a fresh look. Jesus was saying that you should love others more than yourself and be willing to die for them. An agape or selfless, sacrificial, and unconditional love: a Jesus love.

> John 15:13: "Greater love has no one than this, than to lay down one's life for his friends" (NKJV).

The key to a responsible routine is to walk in the Spirit. The part I love about the first scripture (Galatians 5:16) is the word walk (the translation I used says guide, but NKJV says walk). That means you cannot be a spectator watching, but you must do!

On a team, everyone has a part. Someone right now is saying, "But I just stand on the sidelines and cheer." Well, I need you to open your eyes and see the bigger picture. If it was not for you being at practice, those playing would not be successful. On God's team, you cannot be jealous of other's gifts or blessings, because each person has a part in the body of Christ. You are on one team and you receive the same reward as everyone else in the end: ETERNAL LIFE. So make the choice today that you are going to get up, stop making excuses, and walk for God.

By the end of this book you will no longer be a pessimist, always thinking that the glass is half empty, but an optimist, thinking "I can do all things through Christ who strengthens me" (Philippians 4:13, NKJV). Some of you may be thinking, "I do not have a team." I thank God that you do not have to walk alone, that He is there to strengthen you. The next part of the scripture discusses the Spirit. God has given you the Holy Spirit to walk with you along your journey.

> John 14:16-17: "And I will ask the Father, and he will give you another Advocate, who will never leave you. He is the Holy Spirit, who leads into all truth. The world cannot receive him, because it isn't looking for him and doesn't recognize him. But you know him, because he lives with you now and later will be in you" (NLT).

> John 14:26: "But when the Father sends the Advocate as my representative—that is, the Holy Spirit—he will teach you everything and will remind you of everything I have told you" (NLT).

When you are filled with the Spirit, you will not bow down to the lust of the flesh. Your desire to be responsible or trustworthy will be greater than your desire to do wrong. Will you be perfect? No. Will you still mess up sometimes? Yes. The key is that doing right will far outweigh doing wrong. Sin will no longer have control of your life, but the Spirit will. You will go from smoking three cigarettes a day to three a month, and then to none at all. You will go from having sex once a week, to once every other month, to asking for repentance or waiting for the one you want to marry and doing it in a way that is pleasing to God. This is the responsible routine!

This routine is possible with school, playing sports, keeping a job, and seeing that hot guy with a cut-off shirt or that sexy woman in a short summer dress. It is possible because you have chosen God and been saved. You have read the word of God, equipped yourself with the armor of God, and passed tests that have made you stronger in the Lord. So as you continue to mature—no matter your age—make sure you keep the people around you that God has put there and remove the ones you have put there who are choking the life and purpose out of you.

Look back at Matthew 22:37-40 and John 13:34. If you love God like this, it will be easier to love your neighbor. Yes, even the ones that talk about you (Matthew 5:43-44 in NKJV discusses this). Someone is watching you every day and the question is, what are they seeing? The guiding/walking of the Spirit or the lust of the flesh? Read Galatians 5:22-23, Philippians 4:8, and 2 Peter 1:5-8 in NLT. Let these verses take root in your heart and see the guiding/walking of the Spirit. Pray every day that God will show you how to live out the fruit of the Spirit and that He will allow this fruit to work through you in every situation.

> ➢ Psalm 119:11: "Your word I have hidden in my heart, That I might not sin against You" (NKJV).

## Chapter 7 — The Game

### Butterflies

Now it was time for the ultimate test! It was time for the day that all of us had dreamed about since we were kids. You sat at home watching it on TV every Saturday from early afternoon until it was time to go to bed at night. You had parties and gatherings just to watch the best of the best play for two and a half hours. And as you grew up, you met friends and went out to restaurants that had the big game on their TVs. Yes, you guessed right; it was time for COLLEGE GAME DAY!

I remember waking up that day like it was yesterday. I was excited, nervous, and a whole bunch of other emotions all together. I was excited to play in my first college game ever. I was hopeful that I would get into the game as a receiver and catch my first pass as a receiver EVER. But if that did not happen, I at least knew that I would catch a ball as the starting kickoff returner. I was a little nervous and I felt like I was learning to ride a bike for the first time, even though I had been playing football since fifth grade. The one thing I did know was that regardless of how I felt, the game was going to happen.

### Game Routine

Before every game, whether we were home or away, we had a team breakfast. If you know me at all, I don't miss too many meals and I definitely don't miss breakfast. It is the meal that jump-starts your whole day. I did not know what to expect as I had my first team breakfast. We met in one of the cafeterias on campus and sat at tables according to positions. The coach would give us a short talk and then we would eat. Oh my Lord, did I ever eat. We had pancakes, eggs, bacon, sausage, hash browns, cereal, fruit, toast, bagels, and sometimes waffles. Some people were not breakfast eaters, but on game day they ate because they knew how important it was to prepare them for the game and give them the fuel they needed to compete. Once we were done eating, we could go to the locker room or go home and nap or watch ESPN.

I had to be back at the locker room to report in and for taping pretreatments I might have needed due to injuries. Ever since I was in high school, I got my wrist taped and my ankles taped. If you were a receiver or a running back, they recommended that you have your ankles taped. Watching the guys walking around doing their pregame routine to get mentally ready for the game was an amazing environment.

There was an audio system in our locker room and different CDs to get us ready for the game. Some guys had their own headphones and listened to their music, while others just sat, resting and thinking of what needed to be done for the day. After being taped, I would get dressed quickly and get loose while listening to music that was playing. I had prepared all week, so if I was not ready by now, then I never would be. I was serious about the task at hand and thinking about what I needed to do, but I got hyped (as we use to say) to the music. I did not want to be too serious and tense.

The hour was getting closer and closer. The coaches started coming into the locker room. They were seeing how the atmosphere was and if we were ready. The special teams coach called for the first group to hit the field. Yes, that meant me. It was time. I finally got to run out of the tunnel for the first time. I had been waiting for this day for years. You see it on TV when the players run out, but to experience it was breathtaking! Our tunnel was long. It had rubber stoppers going down the entire tunnel so that when you walked with your cleats, you did not fall.

Once we reached the bottom of the tunnel and the fans saw us, one of the upperclassmen circled us up, said a few words, started a chant, and then we broke the huddle loud and proud with DAWGS! And then we were off onto the field.

Once special teams was done warming up on the field, the rest of the team came down the tunnel and stayed at the edge of the tunnel. We then went over to meet them so we could all come out together to stretch. Just thinking about it brings a big smile to my face. It was such a great and sunny day to take the college football field for the first time on a Saturday afternoon game. One of the dreams I had envisioned came true on that Saturday. My parents were in the crowd. Friends and other athletes were in the crowd cheering, students were there, alumni were there; it was just an amazing feeling.

Of course, while we were out there doing special teams and about to stretch and do our pregame warm-up, the opponent was out there too. It was awesome. You had coaches from both teams watching the quarterbacks and the best players, seeing what the other was doing. Students from the other school knew your name and would make comments to distract you. My freshman year I did not get much of that, but I did my sophomore year and a lot my junior and senior years.

The players from the opposing team would start talking trash. They would be trying to intimidate you and make you scared. I heard that in high school, so they were not saying anything I had not already heard. The enemy, Satan, will also try to use past tactics to scare you, but stand firm on God's word. I always thought it was funny, especially since a lot of times it was people who did not even play, but sat on the bench.

Once we were done with our pregame position drills and completed our team run-through, we headed back up to the locker room. This is when it got real. Music was off, everyone was hyping each other up, and it was time to get to work. I had about ten minutes or so to get water and do whatever else I needed to do before we took the field. Coaches would go over any changes and ensure you knew the game plan. Finally, the head coach would come in and give his speech and then we would circle up and pray.

After that, everyone was yelling all the way until we got to the end of the tunnel. One of our team captains was in the middle of the circle giving us a speech about the first game and then we broke the huddle and ran out onto the field. There is nothing like the atmosphere of a college venue: the crowd screaming for their team, the smell of the field, and the feel of the football. YES, YES, YES, IT WAS TRULY GAME TIME!

## Game On

The captains took their spot with the referees on the field to see who would receive the ball or play defense first. My freshman year we had such a mighty offense, we always wanted the ball first. I was more than okay with that because that meant I got the ball since I was the kick returner. I don't remember exactly, but I want to say that we did win the toss and we got the ball first.

I remember my coach yelling, "Kick return team on me." Before a team went on the field we always huddled up with that coach. This was to make sure that we had everyone we needed on the field. We all ran out on the field and the whistle blew. The game had officially started. I do not remember if the ball was kicked to me or not, but I do know that I was very successful at kick returning. I even received a certificate for player of the week with 243 kick return yards and a touchdown in a single game.

Now it was time for our offense to go to work. One thing we must understand is that for an offense to work, it takes all positions doing their part. In this section, I would like to talk a little about some of my transitions that I went through while playing, but I want to focus mostly on the importance of each individual position and how it comes together to make an offense work. If you play defense, do not skip this section. The point is that it takes everyone working together to be successful.

So let's talk about the quarterback (QB) first. The QB, whether he wants to be or not, is the leader of the offense. If you do not have a strong QB who is confident, knowledgeable, and a positive motivator who has a great work ethic and stays late to work with others and the coaching staff, then your offense will not run at its **full** potential. The QB is the one who has to know the opponent's defense better than they do. The QB must know the plays so well that he knows when to make an audible (change a play) because the other team is in a defense that would make the play unsuccessful. Sometimes a team will set up in a defense, disguise it, and then change it right before the QB hikes the ball. From watching their film, the QB must know when a team usually does this. Do they do it when we are in a certain formation, when it is a certain down, when they have a certain player in, or when they are in a certain defense?

The QB must also know all of the signals. These signals are how the offensive coach sends in a play from the sidelines. If the QB misreads a signal, he could call a play that could lose us yards and waste a down. The QB and the offensive coach have to be on the same page. The only way for them to be on the same page is to spend a lot of time together working on signals and timing, and also looking at film and building a trusting relationship. When these two are on the same page, the rest of the offense flows smoothly.

Even though every player should know where to line up, the QB has to know where every position should be on the field. When the offense breaks the huddle, or if the offense does a no huddle, the QB is responsible for making sure that every player is in the right spot before he says "hike." Just like a point guard has to know all the plays, just like a pitcher has to know how many outs, the QB has to know all of this and be able to do it before the play clock runs out. A QB does not develop these skills overnight. A QB has to do his due diligence and work day in and day out to make sure he knows his team's game plan, as well as the other team's game plan.

Lastly, the QB has to complete the play. After he has looked at what the defense is in, has made sure that all of his players are lined up correctly, has checked the time on the play clock, has looked at the coach one last time to make sure he does not want the play changed, he then must hike the ball and hand it off or throw it. It is during this point where natural instincts come into play. Once the QB says "hike," his goal is to get a first down or a touchdown. So, the QB may have to make a tough throw, keep it and run, throw it out of bounds and be smart, or scramble and keep the play alive. However the QB gets it done, he is the commander-in-chief and he must act like it from the first day of practice, to the last game, and during the off-season. If you cannot handle this type of maturity and responsibility, do not be a QB.

The next position I want to discuss is the offensive line (OL). It has been said that the real work happens in the trenches with the OL. The OL is made up of the center, guards, tackles, and a tight end. Depending on the play, there may be two tight ends in the game. Each offensive lineman has a specific assignment and must communicate to each other who they are blocking on each play. Yes, I know, this means the defensive lineman knows on some occasions who will be blocking him. Let me add this: as Christians, we must speak the word of God so the enemy can hear his defeat! Offensive linemen have no excuse for why they missed the blocks because they know who they have to cover. Some teams will come up with different code words for who they are blocking so that the defense does not know who will be blocking them. Regardless, the OL has to make the block for the offense to succeed.

At times the OL will block a gap rather than a person, depending on the play. The key is for the OL to stay disciplined regardless of whether the defense is running a stunt or not. The defense will try to move their linemen around to make the offensive linemen confused so that they can sack the quarterback or disrupt the timing of the play.

The success of the OL has to do with their stance and hand position. They must stay low and get their hands inside to be able to drive the defensive linemen off the line of scrimmage. If the OL put their hands outside of the defensive line's pads, they will be called for a holding penalty. When you are in the trenches, POSITIONING IS EVERYTHING! The OL also must come off the ball quickly. The offense knows the snap count, but the defense does not. So the offense must come off the ball quick, hard, and low.

I use to tell my linemen, "Just get me a yard or two past the line of scrimmage and I'll do the rest!" I always made sure to appreciate and thank my OL. The running back tends to get almost all the publicity. However, if not for the OL, we would never make it past the line of scrimmage. If not for them throwing their bodies in front of the defensive line, the quarterback would be eating grass the entire game. So the OL is like the frontline of an army—they set the tone for how the battle will go.

Next are the brave receivers. You may ask, "Why do you call them brave?" Well, I call them brave because at Butler University I was made a receiver for the first half of the season. It is one thing to watch and see what receivers do, but it is another thing to train, practice, and be a receiver. Depending on the play, the tight end and the running back may be called on to be a receiver.

First and foremost, a receiver has to have confidence. Receivers already know that there is a defensive back (a corner and safety) and a linebacker ready to take them out if they cross in front of them. You cannot be a great receiver and at the same time be worried, afraid, or scared of being hit. You have to have your mind made up and know that being hit is part of the position. Once you have that in your mind, the confidence can start to show. Regardless of what the defensive backs (DB) and linebackers may say, or how they may taunt you, you do not let that bother you because you are confident in yourself and the abilities that you are endowed with to be great at being a receiver.

Next, a receiver has to have faith and trust in his QB. The QB has the power to help keep the receiver a little more protected based upon where he throws the ball. If the QB throws the ball toward the receiver's shoulders or lower, this keeps the receiver's body more protected when he takes a hit. However, if the QB throws the ball above the receiver's head or higher than this, it exposes the receiver's body to a bad hit. This is why a receiver must trust that the QB will throw the ball on time and in the right location so that he can be protected, but also that he can run and advance the ball after the catch.

A receiver must also depend on his skills to get open. Having speed is important, but more than speed, receivers have to know how to put a move on the DB. Receivers know where they need to run, but the DB does not. Because they have been practicing during spring ball, double sessions, and all week, the QB also knows when he wants to throw the receiver the ball and where. So it is up to the receiver to make a move to get himself open so that the play can be successful.

The receiver and QB must have great communication and unity. There will be times when the defense lines up in coverage where the QB will have to audible the play. Usually the QB will audible and change the play so everyone knows. But sometimes it may be a hand code or a look they have practiced to that one receiver. This is why repetition and working together after practice are so important. It is during this repetition that you are prepared for the game itself and the obstacles that may be thrown your way during the game.

Finally, the receiver has to have a great work ethic. Receivers have to know how to get out of a jam. This is when the DB is playing right at the line of scrimmage and receivers have to be quick, get open, and not let the DB get into their pads to keep them from their route. A receiver has to know when to break his route short because the defense is in a zone or has two deep safeties. A receiver has to know when to break the route, scramble, and get open when the QB has to scramble out of the pocket. As equally as important as any of this is, the one thing that keeps the chains moving and the team getting first downs is catching the ball. All of these other skills are important, but if the receiver does not catch the ball, everything else is for nothing.

This is where it is very important for the receiver to work on drills that involve eye and hand coordination skills. One drill is hooking the bungee cord that is attached to a ball to a fence, throwing the ball away from the fence so that it springs back to you, and then you have to catch it. Another drill is standing with your back to the QB or someone who can throw you the ball, then that person throws the ball and says "turn." The receiver has to snap around quickly and find the ball and then catch it. The point is that you have to work very hard on your own so that you are ready during the game.

And for the best position of them all: THE running back (RB). Okay, do not stop reading here because I said that. I had to say that because that is the position I have played my whole life. I must say, if you know you are great at one position, do not let anyone tell you differently, and learn that position to the best of your ability. I am not saying that you should not learn other positions, but sometimes learning other positions can distract you from developing even more in the position you were created to be in.

As I have already stated, I agreed to be a receiver in college and ended up a running back in the middle of my

81

freshman season. Had I been firm and stayed at running back, I could have been an even better player my freshman year. All I am saying is have confidence and faith that the skills you possess in that position are ENOUGH. Again, moving positions may be beneficial, but when you are **given the option as I was**, I knew I was supposed to be an RB!

To be a great RB you must have speed, agility, strength, and great instincts. Most of the time, the RB is the fastest person on the team. I know from experience and I thank God for my speed because I had guys who were 50 to 150 pounds more than me trying to tackle me. It was the speed that got me away from those trying to pursue me.

In order to keep and enhance your speed, you must work hard during the off season. One way to help with your speed is through agility drills. These drills not only help your balance and your footwork, but they also help strengthen the muscles in your legs to become faster. In high school, I was blessed with the chance to work out at Caritas and Sports Acceleration, which were two places whose focus was to make you faster and stronger. After I finished each program, I became a better, faster, and stronger RB.

However, it does not stop there. During practice, you must work hard. After practice you must work with your QB and push yourself to the max in the weight room. To be the best, you must practice the best. From high school to college, I wanted to be first in every drill. As a freshman in college, I wanted to make the upperclassmen look bad and beat them in sprints at the end of practice. Reflecting on this now, I know it's important to make sure your focus is not on making them look bad. Your focus should be on doing your best, which will hopefully push others to get better. When you have that mindset, you cannot do anything but get faster and better.

Agility is so important, because that skill alone can take you from a 1-yard gain to a first down or a touchdown. As I was growing up, I sometimes wondered, *What is the purpose of this drill?* I remember holding the ball in one hand and having to touch the ground with the other hand as if you were falling in a game and doing that for 20 yards. I remember going through the ropes/tires and high stepping. I remember going through the tire gauntlet and at other times going through a gauntlet of players swiping at the ball trying to make you fumble. I thought to myself, *I know they are trying to take this from me, how does this help?* I remember having to go up to a sled and drive it, even though I was not a lineman.

I mention these because now looking back, EVERY ONE of these drills was important. I remember games where I had to catch myself with my hand and push back up to keep going. I had to run through the middle and keep both hands on the ball because linebackers were trying to swipe at the ball. Even though I did not want to block, I had to learn how to stand in the gap, block, and drive that guy back so the play could be successful. Sometimes as an RB you can be so focused on running the ball that you don't realize the other things you need to be successful.

That is why it is so important to listen to your coach, because it is all a process to prepare you for game time situations. He knows what it takes for you to succeed in the game, and it is up to you to listen, follow his directions, and then practice it. You may be wondering why your parent/guardian has you doing this or why that situation happened to you, but just know God is guiding it all, just like the coach was guiding the drills that prepared me for the game.

Another area that is vital to an RB being successful is strength. I came to truly realize how important this was my junior year in high school. I did not play basketball that year so that I could be in the weight room preparing for my senior year. I had such a terrific junior year because I had physically prepared my body for what it would endure that year. One thing

I came to realize when I got to college is that every muscle is important to your success. As guys, we like to focus more on the muscles that are from our abs and up. This is the area that the ladies see most as well as us when we look in the mirror.

But as an RB, your legs are just as important if not more important than your upper body. Your legs are where your power comes from. If you want to be able to break that tackle or drive that huge defensive end back, you must drive with those legs. It was not until college that I realized how far behind I was on my lower body strength. Pound for pound in high school and most of my college career, I was the strongest or within the top three when it came to bench pressing. But when it came to legs, I was one of the weakest. So if you are in middle school or high school, focus on a **complete** physical approach and not just the arms, chest, and abs.

Lastly, you have to have good instincts. Instinct is a natural or innate impulse. This is something that just comes natural. For example: Adrian Peterson may run to the right because that is the way the play was called, and then suddenly you may see him stop and cut left, all the while wondering what is he doing. All the blockers are to the right. Well before you know it, he has a 20-yard gain or a touchdown. That is instinct.

As an RB, you must have this trait and develop it. One way to help develop this trait is to watch film on the other team so you can see how the linebackers, safeties, and corners play and flow to the ball. Another example is that sometimes an RB has to block for the QB. The play is not designed for the RB to go out into a route, but as the QB is on the run, the RB slips out and the QB throws the ball. To summarize instincts: it is when that player you are watching does something that makes you say "WOW!" That is why I think the RB is the greatest position—because we have a lot of WOW moments.

## REFLECTION

Reaching a goal can be exciting and overwhelming. How did you handle reaching your goal? Did you have a humble spirit? Will you stop after you reach your goal or set another goal? These are things that can only be found out when you get off the bench and play the game.

## FAITH WALK

In order to be ready for game day, you must be mentally ready. You should have paid attention to the coaches and scouting report, you should feel confident in yourself and team, and you must trust the coach's game plan. Everything that has happened to me up to this point has led me to where I am today. I have made some good choices and some bad choices, but I thank God that because of His mercy and grace, the good choices far outweigh the bad. What I love about God is that He allowed some good and bad things to happen to me based on my decisions. There are consequences to our decisions and these consequences can be positive or negative. There are some mistakes and sins that I have committed where God's loving kindness has covered me and protected me and no one knows but God and me.

> ➢ Lamentations 3:22-23: "The faithful love of the Lord never ends! His mercies never cease. Great is his faithfulness; his mercies begin afresh each morning" (NLT).

Through my journey, I have realized that I must look at the big picture when making decisions, and not just look at the right now. I had to ask myself, "Is this decision glorifying God?" And if so, I know the consequences will be good. I said all of that to show the process it took to get there. The game is won because of the preparation, practice, studying, and enduring through the unexpected trials. It is also good to note here that sometimes within the process, God Himself will give you a test to bring about the faith and character you need for where He is taking you and the challenges you will face! At first you may ask, "Why, God?" However, as you grow in maturity, you start to say, "THANK YOU, GOD!"

Now that you have developed a steady routine, you must use the power that is in you to help you mentally. Now that you are serious about God, your opponent the devil is going to try to throw obstacles and distractions in your way. He will try to bring up past hurts and failures. He will try to create strife in a relationship and he will try to tempt you with things so you are not focused on the word of God. But thanks be to God that He has a word for this.

> ➢ 2 Corinthians 10:3-5: "We are human, but we don't wage war as humans do. We use God's mighty weapons, not worldly weapons, to knock down the strongholds of human reasoning and to destroy false arguments. We destroy every proud obstacle that keeps people from knowing God. We capture their rebellious thoughts and teach them to obey Christ" (NLT).

First you must realize that you are flesh and bone, but you do not fight according to your flesh. I once heard a pastor say, "If you are struggling that is a good thing. If there is no struggle that is bad." What he was saying is that if we do wrong with no struggle, we have given in to that sin and it has possibly become a stronghold. Read Romans 7:14-25 in NLT.

> ➢ James 1:14-15: "Temptation comes from our own desires, which entice us and drag us away. These desires give birth to sinful actions. And when sin is allowed to grow, it gives birth to death" (NLT).

However, if you are struggling to do wrong, it means the Spirit in you is battling with the flesh.

> ➢ James 4:7-8: "Therefore submit to God. Resist the devil and he will flee from you. Draw near to God and He will draw near to you. Cleanse *your* hands, *you* sinners; and purify *your* hearts, *you* double-minded" (NKJV).

So, as we discussed in the last chapter, you have to walk in the Spirit and let the Spirit have control. Yes, that means you won't have control and you will have to practice self-control, but be assured that with God all things are possible.

> Matthew 19:26: "But Jesus looked at *them* and said to them, 'With men this is impossible, but with God all things are possible'" (NKJV).

> John 15:5: "I am the vine, you *are* the branches. He who abides in Me, and I in him, bears much fruit; for without Me you can do nothing" (NKJV).

This goes back to Matthew 18:18. I love how this is written in the Amplified Classic Version:

> "Truly I tell you, whatever you forbid *and* declare to be improper and unlawful on earth must be what is already forbidden in heaven, and whatever you permit *and* declare proper and lawful on earth must be what is already permitted in heaven."

As a child of God, you have the spiritual authority to speak and pray and when you declare His word, which is His will, God will move on your behalf.

> Matthew 6:10: "Your kingdom come. Your will be done on earth as *it is* in heaven" (NKJV).

It may not happen when you think, but keep praying and believing and in God's time He will show (manifest) His power. It is kind of like asking your parent(s) for something; you usually ask more than once. With God, you must believe and continue to earnestly pray knowing that God hears you and will move. Please read John 14:13-14 in NKJV.

In 2 Corinthians 10, which I shared at the start of this chapter, a word that you must look at that you may not have paid much attention to is "war." A definition of war is a period of armed conflict. A battle is an extended contest or struggle. You must realize that in this war there are going to be many battles.

That is why you have to be continually sharpening your spiritual weapons so that you are ready every time.

> 2 Corinthians 2:11: "lest Satan should take advantage of us; for we are not ignorant of his devices" (NKJV).

In the verses prior to this one, the church brought punishment upon a man as required in that time. The man repented, yet after doing so, the Corinthian church did not receive him back. Paul explains to the church that they should comfort, love, and forgive him. The verse I mentioned is important because Satan would try to make you believe that you should not forgive. But if God tells you to practice forgiveness and you do not, He will not forgive you. Read more about this in Matthew 6:14-15 in NLT. The enemy is looking for any opportunity to take advantage of your mistakes. Because of the Holy Spirit, Satan cannot outwit you; therefore, you are able to be aware of his tactics. The ultimate piece of information to remember is that even though there is a war taking place because of Jesus Christ's sacrifice on the cross, you can have victory over every battle. You just make sure that you call on the name of Jesus during every battle, and watch God work it out!

The next thing you must realize is that verses 4 and 5 have to do with the mind, including strongholds, arguments, and thoughts. You may have allowed strongholds, arguments, and thoughts to fester for years, defining you. Until now, you may not have realized they were driving you to be less than what God created you to be.

> Jeremiah 1:5: "I knew you before I formed you in your mother's womb. Before you were born I set you apart and appointed you as my prophet to the nations" (NLT).

The Lord is speaking to Jeremiah, but God has called you for a great purpose as well. This is why you are not a mistake. Others can say things or make comments that make you feel like a mistake. Regardless of what negative words your mother, father, guardian, or anyone has said, God has a plan and purpose for your existence. You may have been born from unusual circumstances, but God allowed you to be born because He formed you and wants you to know Him so He can guide you to your destiny!

> ➢ Jeremiah 29:11: "For I know the thoughts that I think toward you, says the Lord, thoughts of peace and not of evil, to give you a future and a hope" (NKJV).

> ➢ Psalms 139:13-18: "You made all the delicate, inner parts of my body and knit me together in my mother's womb. Thank you for making me so wonderfully complex! Your workmanship is marvelous—how well I know it. You watched me as I was being formed in utter seclusion, as I was woven together in the dark of the womb. You saw me before I was born. Every day of my life was recorded in your book. Every moment was laid out before a single day had passed. How precious are your thoughts about me, O God. They cannot be numbered! I can't even count them; they outnumber the grains of sand! And when I wake up, you are still with me!" (NLT).

What you must do as a child of God is ask Him and He will reveal His will for your life. Within God revealing His will, you must then walk by faith, trusting that He will get you there.

> ➢ Matthew 7:7-11: "Keep on asking, and you will receive what you ask for. Keep on seeking, and you will find. Keep on knocking, and the door will be opened to you. For everyone who asks, receives. Everyone who seeks, finds. And to everyone who knocks, the door will be opened. You parents—if your children ask for a loaf of bread, do you give them a stone instead? Or if they ask for a fish, do you give them a snake? Of course not! So if you sinful people know how to give good gifts to your children, how much more will your heavenly Father give good gifts to those who ask him" (NLT).

➤ 1 John 5:14-15: "Now this is the **confidence** that we have in Him, that if we ask anything according to His will, He hears us. And if we know that He hears us, whatever we ask, we know that we have the petitions that we have asked of Him" (NKJV).

➤ James 1:5: "If any of you lacks wisdom, you should ask God, who gives generously to all without finding fault, and it will be given to you" (NIV).

The key to asking is to remember that everything is according to God's will and not your own selfish desires, so you must ask with faith and you must keep on knocking. Do not just pray once, but keep seeking Him until He reveals it to you. Be open to how He shows you the answer and take your expectations and limitations off yourself. You sometimes come up with how you want your prayer to be solved, expect it to happen just that way, and you miss the answer God has given you because He gave the solution to you differently than what you had pre-decided.

If the enemy can keep your mind distracted, you cannot focus or clearly hear God speaking. You are killing old habits that have grown and planting new ones that are of God.

➤ Isaiah 43:18-19: "But forget all that—it is nothing compared to what I am going to do. For I am about to do something new. See, I have already begun! Do you not see it? I will make a pathway through the wilderness. I will create rivers in the dry wasteland" (NLT).

These new habits will be rooted in your heart so that you think, say, and do what you know is right.

➤ Proverbs 4:23: "Above all else, guard your heart, for everything you do flows from it" (NIV).

➤ Matthew 12:33-35: "A tree is identified by its fruit. If a tree is good, its fruit will be good. If a tree is bad, its fruit will be bad. You brood of snakes! How could evil men like you speak what is good and right? For whatever is in your heart determines what you say. A good person produces good things from the treasury of a good heart, and an evil person produces evil things from the treasury of an evil heart" (NLT).

Now that you have pulled these proud, high thoughts down, you have dominion over them by bringing them obedient to Christ. You do this by thinking about things spiritually and by *exercising* what you believe so that it becomes a routine.

> Colossians 3:1-2: "Since you have been raised to new life with Christ, set your sights on the realities of heaven, where Christ sits in the place of honor at God's right hand. Think about the things of heaven, not the things of earth" (NLT).

> James 1:16-17: "So don't be misled, my dear brothers and sisters. Whatever is good and perfect is a gift coming down to us from God our Father, who created all the lights in the heavens. He never changes or casts a shifting shadow" (NLT).

> 1 Timothy 4:7-8: "Do not waste time arguing over godless ideas and old wives' tales. Instead, train yourself to be godly. Physical training is good, but training for godliness is much better, promising benefits in this life and in the life to come" (NLT).

If you do this, you will see blessings now and in eternity.

After you are mentally ready for life's challenges, you must heed the words of God.

> Proverbs 2:6: "For the Lord gives skillful *and* godly Wisdom; from His mouth come knowledge and understanding" (AMPC).

God did not create you and leave you wandering aimlessly without a map. The Bible is your road map for how you should live and act, and it provides the spiritual tools you need to do this. I am amazed all the time at how everything that is in the Bible, such as lying, killing, incest, sexual perversion, and other sins, happened back then and continues to happen now. I see how those ordinary people were supernaturally blessed and I know that God can and will do the same for you today. Please read Hebrews 13:8 in NLT. Seek God's understanding and read His word daily. As you do, you will see doors start to open and understanding start to take place. You will go from feeling empty and lost to feeling filled and victorious.

> Psalm 1:1-3: "Oh, the joys of those who do not follow the advice of the wicked, or stand around with sinners, or join in with mockers. But they delight in the law of the Lord, meditating on it day and night. They are like trees planted along the riverbank, bearing fruit each season. Their leaves never wither, and they prosper in all they do" (NLT).

A quick side note, when you are witnessing to friends, pray for them before you go to witness.

> 1 Corinthians 2:14: "But people who aren't spiritual can't receive these truths from God's Spirit. It all sounds foolish to them and they can't understand it, for only those who are spiritual can understand what the Spirit means" (NLT).

This verse tells you that it is not that the person does not want to know about God, but they do not understand because there is so much confusion since they do not have the Holy Spirit. A good book to read on this subject is *Praying Effectively for the Lost* by Lee E. Thomas. I mention this because you are speaking God's word to them, which is powerful. As you pray for unbelief, among other things, to come down, God will start to open their understanding. As you continue to witness (but not pressure them, as actions speak louder than words), they will come because you are planting a seed. The Holy Spirit will draw them and God will bring salvation.

> 1 Corinthians 3:5-7: "After all, who is Apollos? Who is Paul? We are only God's servants through whom you believed the Good News. Each of us did the work the Lord gave us. I planted the seed in your hearts, and Apollos watered it, but it was God who made it grow.

It's not important who does the planting, or who does the watering. What's important is that God makes the seed grow" (NLT).

So now that you are mentally ready and have listened to instruction, you must now implement and trust the game plan and those who God has put in your path to help you.

> Proverbs 3:5-6: "Lean on, trust in, *and* be confident in the Lord with all your heart and mind and do not rely on your own insight *or* understanding. In all your ways know, recognize, *and* acknowledge Him, and He will direct *and* make straight *and* plain your paths" (AMPC).

Because of everything you have done up to this point and how you have allowed God, the Holy Spirit, and the blood of Jesus to work in you, now you are able to walk a straighter path and to lean more towards God than towards your flesh.

The first thing you see in these scriptures that you must do is TRUST in the Lord. Just like you have to trust the coaches and the game plan, you have to trust the Lord's plan for your life. His plan is for you to prosper, to live life more abundantly, to witness to others, to give Him glory, and to do great things for the Kingdom of God. While you are trusting the Lord, there will be difficulties that arise to test you, to build your faith, and to deepen your trust in Him.

For example, the coach does not just come up with a game plan to implement on game day. The coach draws up a game plan, tests it out in practice based on film and scouting, and then makes adjustments as needed. God is so, so, so good that He won't just throw you out there without making sure you are ready and prepared. God has already drawn up the plan for you. He is now testing you to mature you so that you will not mess up the blessing He is going to give you, and the Holy Spirit in you will give you the help you need to make the adjustments.

> James 1:2-4: "Dear brothers and sisters, when troubles of any kind come your way, consider it an opportunity

for great joy. For you know that when your faith is tested, your endurance has a chance to grow. So let it grow, for when your endurance is fully developed, you will be perfect and complete, needing nothing" (NLT). Once God knows He can trust you, be ready for the magnificent blessings that He will shower upon you. Again I refer to Proverbs.

> Proverbs 3:5-6: "Lean on, trust in, *and* be confident in the Lord with all your heart *and* mind and do not rely on your own insight *or* understanding" (AMP).

There is that word heart again. By now you ought to realize that the heart is very important. You have probably heard a coach or parent say, "I just have a gut feeling about this." For the Christian, it is not a gut feeling, but the Holy Spirit working in you, giving you guidance. The Holy Spirit pulls this guidance out of your heart where you have hidden the word of God.

> Psalms 119:11: "Your word I have hidden in my heart, That I might not sin against You" (NKJV).

> Proverbs 4:4: "He also taught me, and said to me: 'Let your heart retain my words; Keep my commands, and live'" (NKJV).

> Proverbs 4:20-23: "My child, pay attention to what I say. Listen carefully to my words. Don't lose sight of them. Let them penetrate deep into your heart, for they bring life to those who find them, and healing to their whole body. Guard your heart above all else, for it determines the course of your life" (NLT).

Before you were saved, your heart was filled with all kinds of worldly desires and habits. Now that you understand how important the heart is and want to get rid of the old lifestyle and habits, you must pray like David:

> Psalms 51:10: "Create in me a clean heart O God, and renew a steadfast spirit within me" (NKJV).

The next word in Proverbs 3:5 I love, as well as in the Bible, is ALL. If I had time I would talk about this word in detail, but this book is not about that. I will give you one scripture.

> Philippians 4:19: "And my God shall supply all your need according to His riches in glory by Christ Jesus" (NKJV).

If you're in His will and you are depending on Him, there is not anything that you cannot do.

> Ephesians 3:20: "Now to him who is able to do immeasurably more than all we ask or imagine, according to his power this is at work within us" (NIV).

> Mark 16:17-18: "These miraculous signs will accompany those who believe: They will cast out demons in my name, and they will speak in new languages. They will be able to handle snakes with safety, and if they drink anything poisonous, it won't hurt them. They will be able to place their hands on the sick, and they will be healed" (NLT).

So as Nike, McDonald's, and my Pastor, Reverend Malone Jr. respectively say, "Just do it," "I'm loving it," and "That is splendiferous!" In other words, when you do God's will and trust Him, you will be amazed at how God will use you.

The word "all" could be defined by: as much as possible. We all like to take credit for our accomplishments. You love to say, "I did it, I came up with that," or "I scored that touchdown," when in reality you did all (as much as possible) you could do, but the Holy Spirit empowered us to have that idea or skill to get that touchdown. When you love and trust the Lord with all your heart, it cannot be a lukewarm action. You cannot be on the fence; you must serve Him fully. You trust God when you are going through something difficult, and then when everything is okay, you go back to serving the world. Regardless of whether you are on the mountain top or in the valley, you must serve and trust the Lord ALL the time.

> Revelations 3:15-16: "I know all the things you do, that you are neither hot nor cold. I wish that you were one or

the other!  But since you are like lukewarm water, neither hot nor cold, I will spit you out of my mouth!" (NLT)

Christ is looking for Christians who are wholeheartedly seeking Him, not halfheartedly.  David was not a perfect man and you will not be either, but the key is to always strive for perfection, which David tried.  Because David was a man after God's heart, he was then promoted to greatness.

> Acts 13:22: "But God removed Saul and replaced him with David, a man about whom God said, 'I have found David son of Jesse, a man after my own heart. He will do everything I want him to do'" (NLT).

Once you trust in the Lord you cannot "lean on your own understanding" anymore.  Any choice you make should now be measured by the word of God, not just by how you feel. Feeling and trusting friends (that truly were not friends) is what got you where you are now.  You must raise your standards and let God lead your life.  You must live for Christ, which is righteousness, and not for the devil, which is a selfish, fleshly desire.  This goes with Proverbs 3:6, which I noted earlier:

> "In all your ways know, recognize, *and* acknowledge Him, and He will direct *and* make straight *and* plain your paths" (AMPC).

 When you trust Him and do it wholeheartedly, you are acknowledging Him.  He will open up the doors for you and bless you.  What we must realize is that we should want more spiritual blessings rather than monetary blessings, which are temporary.

> 2 Corinthians 4:16-18: "Therefore we do not lose heart. Even though our outward *man* is perishing, yet the inward man is being renewed day by day.  For our light affliction, which is but for a moment, is working for us a far more exceeding *and* eternal weight of glory, while we do not look at the things which are seen, but at the things which are not seen.  For the things which are seen

*are* temporary, but the things which are not seen are eternal" (NKJV).

➢ Ephesians 1:3: "Blessed *be* the God and Father of our Lord Jesus Christ, who has blessed us with every spiritual blessing in the heavenly *places* in Christ" (NKJV).

Sometimes, because of the bad nature you were born with, you try to gimmick God. You think, *I'll do right in hopes that I get a car, house, money, or a good man/woman. I'll make the team, get a job, be healed, and my parents will stay together, etc.* God can do all of these things, but He wants to give you spiritual blessings so that you will be ready to carry out the plan He has for you. You have to understand this! It does you no good to get a job if you do not have the peace needed to handle the work and people. There is no need for you to make the team if you do not have the humbleness and character it takes to succeed and handle the pressure. There is no need for you to have a relationship to make you feel better if you do not already have the joy of the Lord on the inside and the self-confidence to know who you are in Christ. You can have all the money or success, yet still feel empty because you are not doing it unto the Lord. Acknowledging Him means that you know you need Him and that you cannot make it without Him.

Now, I want to mention the last part of the verse in Proverbs 3:6 again, which says, "In all your ways know, recognize, *and* acknowledge Him, and He will direct *and* make straight *and* plain your paths" (AMPC). He shall direct your paths is a promise! You have to love that God wants your participation. The God who is all powerful, all-knowing, and ever-present has given you (if you are saved) authority to get things done here on earth. Do not let Jesus' death be for nothing. Start exercising your authority. Some promises are conditional and will only be given if you do your part. In order for Him to direct your paths, you must trust and acknowledge Him with all your heart. If you never remove your selfishness and pride, you won't be able to see the spiritual paths God has made for you.

> 1 Corinthians 2:9: "That is what the scriptures mean when they say, "No eye has seen, no ear has heard, and no mind has imagined what God has prepared for those who love him"" (NLT).

I am excited right now just thinking about the word "paths." God is not just going to direct you onto one path, but multiple paths. Each path He takes you on, He must be the guide or coach.

> Exodus 13:21-22: "The Lord went ahead of them. He guided them during the day with a pillar of cloud, and he provided light at night with a pillar of fire. This allowed them to travel by day or by night. And the Lord did not remove the pillar of cloud or pillar of fire from its place in front of the people" (NLT).

> Joshua 1:5 "No man shall *be able* to stand before you all the days of your life; as I was with Moses, *so* I will be with you. I will not leave you nor forsake you" (NKJV).

I am a living witness that God will keep you and get you to the promises He has told you if you just keep trusting, asking, and believing. I always said it would be neat to write a book, and God would not let that desire in my spirit leave and has enabled me to do it. I know it was God who put that desire in my heart and I thank Him even now for how this book WILL bless, heal, strengthen, and deliver those reading this NOW! My wife has said that she wants to write a book, and I speak that her book will come to pass in Jesus' name.

When my wife and I signed for the house that God told us we could have, we had to make three months' worth of house payments for two houses (the new house and my wife's house at the time). It took faith for us to sign on a new house when we had not sold her house. I hoped her house would have sold sooner, but we trusted God and it ended up selling. The shouting news is that I had just enough money in my savings account for three months of my wife's house payment. So even though I had planned to save that money for something else, God knew how much I needed and when I was going to need it. He is always on time! I could provide you with numerous testimonies, but the key is to trust and have faith even when it does not look like there is an open door. Because God is with you, He will open the door. He may keep it closed because He knows it is not good for you to go through, but he will open the right doors for you. Your responsibility is to take action and walk through it.

Lastly, you have to have confidence and faith in the team and coaching staff in order to win the game. Just as football is not an individual sport, neither is the Christian walk. Let's discuss your coaching staff (God, Jesus, and Holy Spirit), and the team God has given you (Christian friends), who will lead you to victory.

> John 16:12-15: "I still have many things to say to you, but you cannot bear *them* now. However, when He, the Spirit of truth, has come, He will guide you into all truth; for He will not speak on His own *authority*, but whatever He hears He will speak; and He will tell you things to come. He will glorify Me, for He will take of what is Mine and declare *it* to you. All things that the Father has are Mine. Therefore I said that He will take of Mine and declare *it* to you" (NKJV).

These scriptures describe your Christian coaching staff. Let me break it down like this: God is your head coach, Jesus is the offensive coordinator, and the Holy Spirit is the quarterback. They all work together to guide you to victory. Jesus only does what God tells Him to do, and the Holy Spirit declares what Jesus tells Him.

> John 14:10-11: "Do you not believe that I am in the Father, and the Father in Me? The words that I speak to you I do not speak on My own *authority*; but the Father

who dwells in Me does the works. Believe Me that I am in the Father and the Father in Me, or else believe Me for the sake of the works themselves" (NKJV).

Once you are saved, you now have the help of the Holy Spirit working in you. When you feel something is wrong, and you feel uncomfortable doing something or going somewhere you used to, that is not something bad you ate or a gut feeling. It is the Holy Spirit leading you to truth or righteousness.

With a coaching staff like this, you cannot do anything but WIN! This is why you should not be changing plays (audible like a quarterback) without the guidance of the Holy Spirit helping you.

> 1 Corinthians 2:10-14: "But God has revealed *them* to us through His Spirit. For the Spirit searches all things, yes, the deep things of God. For what man knows the things of a man except the spirit of the man which is in him? Even so no one knows the things of God except the Spirit of God. Now we have received, not the spirit of the world, but the Spirit who is from God, that we might know the things that have been freely given to us by God. These things we also speak, not in words which man's wisdom teaches but which the Holy Spirit teaches, comparing spiritual things with spiritual. But the natural man does not receive the things of the Spirit of God, for they are foolishness to him; nor can he know *them*, because they are spiritually discerned" (NKJV).

The Holy Spirit knows what is best for you because He has been in constant fellowship with God and Jesus. So when the Holy Spirit says, "Go straight, go left, go right, stop, turn around, go through that door (a blessing), shut that door (a trap of the enemy), pray, fast, or witness to that person," YOU DO IT! If the Holy Spirit does not tell you to go and does not tell you to say that, then don't.

> Zechariah 4:6: "So he answered and said to me: This is the word of the Lord to Zerubbabel: 'Not by might nor

by power, but by My Spirit,' Says the Lord of hosts" (NKJV).

When you look at the Corinthian scripture from above, you realize that wisdom and knowledge come from God through the Holy Spirit. It only makes sense to me that you should follow the lead of the Holy Spirit because He is getting information for you from God who created you. If He created you and knows the plans for you before you were born, then He will not tell you the wrong information. You must do as Matthew 7:7-11 (NLT) says and ask, seek, and knock. God is ready to reveal the plays and purposes He has for you, but are you ready to receive them? God is looking for players who will study the playbook (word of God), who will practice hard (pray, memorize the word of God, be forgiving and loving), and who will be ready for game day (use spiritual power to advance the Kingdom of God).

Not only do you need to have confidence in your staff, but you must have confidence and trust in your team. I played offense in college at Butler University, so this is why I use offense as my analogy. Now that your eyes have been opened, you are probably starting to see that some of the friends around you are not the friends you need. But be assured that when you remove the wrong ones, God will open your eyes to see the ones that are already in front of you that He has placed there to be a blessing to you.

> Psalms 91:1-2: "Those who live in the shelter of the Most High will find rest in the shadow of the Almighty. This I declare about the LORD: He alone is my refuge, my place of safety; he is my God, and I trust him" (NLT).
> Psalms 91:9-13: "If you make the LORD your refuge, if you make the Most High your shelter, no evil will conquer you; no plague will come near your home. For

he will order his angels to protect you wherever you go. They will hold you up with their hands so you won't even hurt your foot on a stone. You will trample upon lions and cobras; you will crush fierce lions and serpents under your feet!" (NLT).

I was a running back and I had to trust that my linemen were not only going to make the right calls they had to make, but that they were going to hold their blocks so I could gain yards, which would get our team closer to a TD! For you as a Christian, you must trust God and make Him your fortress and refuge. Regardless of what friends turn their backs on you, what bad thing they say about you, what rumor they start, or what pain they have caused you, you must trust God because He will keep you. God has angels watching and protecting; He dispatches them at the time you need them. There was something that was supposed to happen to you and you didn't even know it, but that is because God's angels were protecting you.

Read all of Psalms 91 because it describes how you will dwell or rest in the secret place of God. When you do, nothing will get you frazzled because you will trust more on God and His strength than your own. When you are focused on Him, no defensive lineman (the enemy, Satan) can do anything to stop what God has purposed for you to do. As you rest in that secret place, God is preparing you and maturing you so that you will be ready for the test coming your way and so that you will be ready to walk in the blessing He has for you. And a side note: the secret place is in you, because your body is a temple. The secret place is where you spend time with God in His word and prayer, and due to this, you will find rest. Read Psalm 27:5, Psalm 31:20, and Colossians 1:27 in NIV.

God does not just have heavenly angels watching over you, but He has earthly angels that I call godly friends. I believe that you should pray and ask God to send you godly friends, just like you would pray for everything else. Having the right friends can change your life!  A friend that prays, is optimistic, and practices the word of God will strengthen you, be honest with you, and be an encourager to you.  You shouldn't want to hang with someone because of their popularity status.  You won't get into heaven by being popular, but you will make it there for being righteous.  And as the old saying goes, "You become who you hang with."

So, don't ruin your witness by hanging around drugs, alcoholics, fornicators, gossipers, liars, people that curse, and cheaters just because you want to be cool.  Live by the standards of God and ask Him if this friend is good for you.  When you have a team of friends that are on fire for God, your thinking will change and as a team, you will be able to conquer and do more for God.  This is where you can all witness and help others know Jesus.

> Matthew 18:19-20: "I also tell you this: If two of you agree here on earth concerning anything you ask, my Father in heaven will do it for you.  For where two or three gather together as my followers, I am there among them" (NLT).

Create a new team TODAY.  Dwell in God's secret place daily and watch God allow you to trample over the enemy!

## Chapter 8 — The Victory

### Score to Win

I believe that whatever you do in life, the goal should be to win! Winning is not always measured by wins and losses, but can be measured by personal goals and effort. Let me explain. In order to win, there is always something you have to do or an action you have to take. And whenever you ACT (Action Changes Things), something must follow whether good or bad. Action is something changed by the exertion of power (not ours, but the Holy Spirit in us). Let me say right here, do not let the fear of something bad happening keep you from trying, because trying is a win-win situation. If I try and do well, I WIN! If I try and do poorly, it is an opportunity for me to learn, grow, work harder, and get better. Maybe I thought I was great in a particular area, but after being tested I found a weakness. Now I can practice and make it a strength.

You have to understand this before we go any further. Winning is important, but the losses are what make you appreciate what it takes to win. Once you have won, it is a feeling you want to have ALL THE TIME! So when you lose, it makes you want to work that much harder so that you can get back in the winner's circle. There is something on the inside that won't let you give up and quit because it has tasted the success of winning. When you want to give up, call it quits, or make excuses, a memory of winning appears and pushes you to practice more, dig deep from within, and continue to persevere. If you think of a time you have won, even if it has only been once, remember how it felt and use that to fuel you every day. Do this, and I know you will start to see more wins than losses.

In order to win you have to score. Whatever sport you may play or watch, the team or person has to score in some way. It has been said that it is easy to coach from people on the outside, but until you are the head coach and make game time decisions, it is totally different. When you are watching the game from the outside (in the stands or on TV), it looks like it is very easy to score. When you are looking from the outside, you can see every angle of what is going on and you cannot understand why the players, who are trained and skilled at what they do, are not seeing what you see.

However, when you are in the game and trying to score, there are so many things happening and they are happening at a "right now" pace (much like life). The player(s) and coach must make decisions they feel will bring the best results. At times, you may make a decision based on natural instinct that you did not practice or never tried, but it works because something in you took over. There will also be times where you make a decision and despite all of your hard work and effort, it does not work. Regardless though, the key is to try and score.

## Score a Touchdown

One way you can score in football is to cross the goal line. Crossing the goal line on a play from scrimmage ensures that your team will receive six points. There is nothing more exciting than crossing that goal line and hearing the crowd scream for the team and you. I remember when I played football starting in fifth grade at St. Anthony's. I was one of the smallest, skinniest kids out there, yet I was also one of the fastest. Even though I was fast, I had to get past all the kids who were bigger than me trying to tackle me. Coach Theobald, who is one of the best coaches I have had, would tell me, "Justin, you have to run north and south, not east and west." I understood what Coach was saying and I would run straight until I saw guys coming at me, then I'd run toward the sideline to try to get around them so I could run straight again. The only problem was, they did not make the field wide enough like the length.

Well, that season I remember getting the ball on the right side, getting some good blocks, and scoring. YES, it was my first touchdown ever! I will never forget that day. I felt so alive hearing the crowd, my teammates congratulating me, my coach telling me "way to go," and my parents in the crowd cheering and being proud of me. It was from me continually trying and finally scoring that jump-started my running back career. Had I gotten down on myself, quit, or believed that I would always run east and west, I never would have felt how I felt that day. I am telling you TODAY, it will come. It took me several games to get my first touchdown, but it came. And your score—your touchdown—is going to come. Keep trying, keep running, keep persevering, because there is nothing like a victory that you have fought for and earned yourself!

See, nothing changed physically, but mentally I changed. I was still one of the smallest and skinniest kids, but I wanted that feeling every time I touched the ball. Now, the only way I could get that feeling was to go through the opposition, the bigger players trying to tackle me. Mentally, I was finally willing to take some hits in order to score. If you keep trying and don't give up, something inside will push you to make it through every trial so you can get to your victory!

You can sit on the sidelines and wish you could win, or you can let your actions change things. Make up in your mind, just as I did, to push forward. I did not focus on the times I ran east and west, but I focused on the one time I ran north and south and the results it brought. All you have to do is focus on today and your future. Stop looking backwards, stop carrying the past, and start running forward and cross the goal line. I thank God that, just like in football where you get four downs and a set of new downs every 10 yards, He gives us new mercies every day and another chance because of Jesus' death and resurrection!

## Score a Field Goal

Another way you can score is by kicking a field goal. In football, you receive three points for making a field goal.

Remember, the goal is to win by scoring. So even though kicking a field goal is less than crossing the goal line, the key is you are earning points. You receive these three points by kicking the football in-between the goal posts or the uprights. The kicker must be talented, focused, and ready for the moment.

Let's put this into perspective. To score a touchdown, I have 53.33 yards in width to run and 100 yards in length. However, to score a field goal (according to NCAA standards), the kicker has to kick it in a goal post where the bottom bar is 10 feet from the ground and in-between two posts that are 18 feet and 6 inches apart. If the size of the goal post is not enough, the kicker has to have a good snap by the center, a good hold by the holder, and good blocks by the linemen. He has to tune out the crowd and the opposing team, and he has to plant his foot firm in the ground and kick it through that tiny space for three points. Not to mention, the kicker does not get to choose which side of the field he wants to kick from. He has to kick it from the spot on the field where the last play ended, which is the left hash, the right hash, or the center of the field. The kicker's job becomes even more challenging based on whether this is early in the game or late in the game, how many field goals he has made or missed, if it is a game winner or will take them into overtime, and the weather conditions.

So how does a kicker become consistent? They PRACTICE! Kickers can get a reputation for having it easy or being weak, but those three points are important and can be the difference from a win or loss. The kicker, more than anyone, must have a short-term memory, because it is all about the next kick, not the last kick. If you made the kick, GREAT, but now it is on to the next kick. If you missed a kick, that is okay, now it is on to the next kick.

In practice, the kicker has to move the football all over the field. He has to practice short and long kicks, kicks from the right and from the left, and kicks in the rain, wind, and sunshine.

The kicker has to know how to change the trajectory (height of the football) if someone gets through a block. The kicker also has to know when to yell "fire" (the code word we used when the kick was not possible), scramble, and get a first down or score, depending on where the team is located on the field. All of these scenarios are practiced by the team and kicker before the game.

In your own life, just score. Do not worry if you only get three points instead of six points. The key is you scored. At times, it is harder to get the three points than the six points, so give yourself a pat on the back. Maybe you are the friend of the kicker; give him encouragement and support and let him know that it looks like a tight situation (just like the goal post is tight), but he can do it. Maybe he missed a kick already, but tell him the game is not over, the coach is calling him, and he is up again! Let him know that the coach is not giving up, so do not give up on yourself. Maybe you are the kicker. Well, encourage yourself. Tell yourself, "I have been practicing for this day for months." Tell yourself, "I have had to endure some tough practices that have prepared me for game day." The misses and makes in practice have prepared you for the game of life TODAY! So before you kick it, picture the ball going in the uprights and your team, coaches, and the crowd screaming for you. The key is to see it by faith before it ever happens. Believe it is through the uprights before you ever kick it. What you believe is what you will make happen! Score three and do not let anyone tell you that those three points are not of value.

## Score after the Touchdown

There are two ways you can score after getting a touchdown and crossing the goal line. You can kick an extra point that is worth one point or you can run a play and cross the goal line, which is worth two points. Both of these plays are run from the 3-yard line. The play you choose to run will depend on the situation that you are in during the game.

On most occasions, teams go for the extra point. This means that the field goal team will come on the field and the kicker will kick a 20-yard field goal, which is pretty easy for most kickers. It is 20 yards because the end zone is 10 yards in length, the ball is placed on the 3-yard line, and the holder lines up 7 yards back from the 3-yard line where the ball is placed. From this distance, it is easier to get one point than it is to score a two-point conversion.

A two-point conversion is tough, because you do not have a lot of room to work with. The ball is on the 3-yard line and you have 10 yards of the end zone to work with, but you cannot forget about the defense and all the players that are in that little space. So going for two in such a small space limits some of the calls a coach can make. This is why a team receives two points, because it is more challenging to score. A team may go for two because, when calculating the points they need to win or catch up, they must.

The person who makes this call on whether the team goes for one or two points is the coach. And the team must have complete trust in the coach's decision and then must execute what the coach wants. As we go through the playing field of life, our coach, God, is telling us which direction to go and he leaves it up to us to execute. Just like the coach has given you everything you need to achieve success and score regardless if it is one or two points, God has given us everything we need through the Holy Spirit to be successful and score.

What I need you to understand is after you get the touchdown, do not be satisfied. Just like the game will continue and just like there will be another opponent, you cannot get content with your success. In life, you are going to have some victories, but do not stop there. Keep going and scoring so you ensure that you win. I am sure you have watched a game where your team had the lead or started off good only to lose because they took their foot off the gas. Well, don't allow this to happen to you. Just as there are so many ways to score in football, there are many ways you can score in life. Most of the time you win by helping others win. Do not always think about yourself. Just as a team must help each other, think of how you can help someone. Whether you score a touchdown or a field goal, just keep trying, keep pressing, and keep believing. If you do these things, at the end of the day, VICTORY from your ACTions will always prevail!

## Score Legally

Now some may say, "Well, I understand what you are saying, and I am scoring now that I know how to score." I am glad you are still reading this book, because just as football has rules on how you score, so does life. In football, there are guidelines so that the team on offense does not gain an unfair advantage.

One of these rules is that the player cannot lateral the ball forward once the ball is past the line of scrimmage. Can you imagine how the game of football would be if the quarterback could start running down the field and still throw the ball at any point? Or think if the quarterback threw the ball and then the player who caught the ball could throw the ball forward again. It would be almost impossible for the defense to stop a team. However, you can lateral the football to another player that is beside you or behind you.

A couple examples of this are the hook and ladder, and the option. The hook and ladder is a play where the quarterback throws it to the outside receiver who does a hook pattern. When the receiver catches it, he tosses it to the inside receiver who comes behind him. The option is between the quarterback and the running back. The quarterback can pitch it to the running back behind the line of scrimmage, but he may have to turn up the field sooner than he anticipated. The running back must try to stay with the quarterback, because as long as he stays behind him, the quarterback can still pitch the ball to him. So, just like there are rules that teams must follow, there are rules that we must follow to ensure that we set ourselves up to be successful and win.

Another rule is that once you are down by contact (from an opposing player), you are down and cannot advance the ball any further. Think about a football game you have watched and the offensive player tripped over the defensive player's foot or the defensive player hit the offensive runner's foot and after stumbling for 5 yards, he finally fell. If not for this rule, players would get back up and just keep running. It is because of this rule that blocking is so important and football is such a team sport. Life has a way of trying to tackle you, but if you get the right team around you, they will block for you with prayer and encouragement, and you will once again be successful and win! You are also considered down when your knee or forearm is down, regardless if the defense has touched you (this is not the case in the NFL). In life, we can be moving faster than God and we trip ourselves up.

There have been a couple of incidents where a player or a staff member has hindered a player from scoring a touchdown, such as tripping them going down the sideline. In the moment, that person may have thought that was the right thing to do, but realized later that it was wrong, hurtful to the player, and hurtful to his team. At that point in time, the person may have even thought he was helping his team win, but after receiving negative press attention, realized he made the issue worse. What I am trying to get you to understand is that there are situations in life where you may choose to not follow the rules to get an advantage; however, it is not until later that you realize in the long run it was no advantage at all.

111

Because of what you have seen, breaking the rules may look easier, but what are the life-long results? How far can that take you? What do you have to give up? What people do you have to hurt? What part of you do you give up following this lifestyle? Don't let what you have seen or been introduced to override what you really know in your heart is not you.

Choose to get back in the right game. Choose to follow the rules. As you change, watch the love, support, and success that will follow. It won't be easy, but not being yourself isn't easy either. It takes practice to be a liar, a thief, a drug dealer, a killer, a cutter, a prostitute. It takes courage to write that suicide note, to move out on your own, to sleep around, or to pop pills. You did not start off doing these things, but maybe you thought that was the way to cope with what you were going through.

WELL RIGHT NOW I AM CALLING A TIMEOUT AND THROWING THE RED FLAG! In football, when the coach throws the red flag, that means the play is under review and the call can be changed. I see who you really are and who God created you to be. Today is a new day, a new practice. Today you are going to take the right road, change the plays in your playbook of life, and start to WIN! It is going to take some double sessions (or practice) and some sweat to get back into shape, but know that when you have that first game and you win, NOTHING WILL COMPARE!

Winning does not mean having the most money, awards, or fans, but having joy, peace, and love! You win because you have joy on the inside. You win because you feel good about yourself ALONE! You have gotten to the point where you do not need people to validate you. You validate yourself. You win because you have peace about what you are doing. You don't have to look over your shoulder to see who may be after you because of what you did. You don't have to wonder if your parents know what you did or didn't do, because you are doing the right things. If you are going through life always wondering, always worrying, always looking over your shoulder, it can stop today. I thank God that every day I wake up is another chance for me to get it right. So ask God for forgiveness and then make up your mind that today you are going to move one step closer to peace, which is found in Jesus Christ!

Lastly, give love. Some of us have been taught and told that you only love those who love you. Well, this is not true. At one point, we did not love God and were not thinking about God, yet he sent his son Jesus to die for us. Maybe right now you have not been thinking about God, but guess what? He sent his son for you, too! Yes, put a smile on your face, because today you can know that God loves you. That is why when you know God, you will be able to love others that do not love you. The great joy in this kind of love is that the other person never has any power or control over how you feel.

We get mad when people do not like or love us, but when I know that God loves me, I am not worried about others. So, learn to love others. Put a positive spin on their day and let them wonder why you are so nice to them even though they do not deserve it. Let them ponder how it is that during one season you were one person, but this season you are full of love and goodness! Live a complete life with joy and peace in spite of people, situations, or your past. YES, it's time for you to reap your harvest, right now, in this season!

> 1 Samuel 30:6-8: "David was now in great danger because all his men were very bitter about losing their sons and daughters, and they began to talk of stoning him. But David found strength in the LORD his God. Then he said to Abiathar the priest, 'Bring me the ephod!' So Abiathar brought it. Then David asked the LORD, 'Should I chase after this band of raiders? Will I catch them?' And the lord told him, **'Yes, go after them. You will surely recover everything that was taken from you!'**" (NLT).

➤ 1 Samuel 30:16-20: "So he led David to them, and they found the Amalekites spread out across the fields, eating and drinking and dancing with joy because of the vast amount of plunder they had taken from the Philistines and the land of Judah. David and his men rushed in among them and slaughtered them throughout that night and the entire next day until evening. None of the Amalekites escaped except 400 young men who fled on camels. <u>David got back everything the Amalekites had taken,</u> and he rescued his two wives. Nothing was missing: small or great, son or daughter, nor anything else that had been taken. <u>David brought everything back.</u> He also recovered all the flocks and herds, and his men drove them ahead of the other livestock. 'This plunder belongs to David!' they said" (NLT).

## REFLECTION

Everyone has to decide what success means to them. How do you measure success? Can you handle success? Can you be successful even if you do not win? Now that you have made it to the end zone and tasted victory, other tests will come, but now you know how to make it through!

## FAITH WALK

If you have made it to this point, then pat yourself on the back. Hug yourself and give a loud shout of praise (wherever you are) to God because victory is yours. If you have made it to this chapter, then the new complete you has already begun to take place and I know you can see the effects of it already. As I close this book, I want to make sure you know victory is yours, give you a few stories in the Bible that will help you understand how to have victory, and make sure your confidence and belief is higher than before you started this book.

Victory is yours because of Christ.

> 1 Corinthians 15:57: "But thank God! He gives us victory over sin and death through our Lord Jesus Christ" (NLT).

> 1 John 5:4-5: "For every child of God defeats this evil world, and we achieve this victory through our faith. And who can win this battle against the world? Only those who believe that Jesus is the Son of God" (NLT).

These verses tell you that it is your faith in Christ, the son of God, which allows you to overcome the world. It is Christ's death, burial, and resurrection that give you the victory.

> John 16:33: "I have told you these things, so that in Me you may have [perfect] peace. In the world you have tribulation *and* distress *and* suffering, but be courageous [be confident, be undaunted, be filled with joy]; I have overcome the world. [My conquest is accomplished, My victory abiding]" (AMP).

The question, which by now you should be able to answer is, "Where does your faith lie or who does it lie with?" Prayerfully, you can say in God through the finished work of Jesus Christ.

So, what is faith?

> Hebrews 11:1: "Now faith is the substance of things hoped for, the evidence of things not seen" (NKJV).

> Hebrews 11:6: "But without faith *it is* impossible to please *Him*, for he who comes to God must believe that He is, and *that* He is a rewarder of those who diligently seek Him" (NKJV).

Faith believes and hopes even when you do not see it because of God's word. Verse 6 says, "those who diligently seek Him." To seek Him you must read His word. You may be in a situation where there is no peace, however you will say:

> Isaiah 26:3: "You will keep in perfect *and* constant peace *the one* whose mind is steadfast [that is, committed and focused on You-in both inclination and character], because he trusts *and* takes refuge in You [with hope and confident expectation]" (AMP).

You may feel fear creeping up in your mind so you say and
believe:

> 2 Timothy 1:7: "For God has not given us a spirit of
> fear, but of power and of love and of a sound mind"
> (NKJV).

If there is a teacher, friend, coach, parent, or person who has
made you mad, rather than giving them an attitude, you will
believe God for his supernatural strength while that person is still
in front of you speaking. Why?

> 1 John 4:4: "Little children (believers, dear ones), you
> are of God and you belong to Him and have [already]
> overcome them [the agents of the antichrist]; because He
> who is in you is greater than he (Satan) who is in the
> world [of sinful mankind]" (AMP).
> Nehemiah 8:10b: "Do not sorrow, for the joy of the Lord
> is your strength" (NKJV).

If you read all of Hebrews 11, you will see the faith of others
that trusted God when the situation looked hopeless.

Along with this faith, you need confidence. I thank God
that my parents were there to teach me and encourage me, but at
some point I had to stand on my own two feet. Unfortunately for
some people, they have had to stand on their own two feet
sooner than normal. If this is you, know that God is with you
and He can and will help you as He did with me. God can give
you confidence and the power to do things that are unimaginable
and beyond what you even ask for.

> Ephesians 3:20: "Now all glory to God, who is able,
> through his mighty power at work within us, to
> accomplish infinitely more than we might ask or think"
> (NLT).

Do you not believe me? Well, read the Bible, pray, get in a
church, ask God, be patient, and then let me know if He does not
blow your mind.

> Psalms 34:8: "Oh, taste and see that the Lord *is* good;
> Blessed *is* the man *who* trusts in Him!" (NKJV).

You have tried trusting in people, substances, and things, yet nothing has worked or brought you satisfaction. You have nothing to lose and everything to gain. Try and trust Jesus!

> ➢ Hebrews 3:12-14: "Be careful then, dear brothers and sisters. Make sure that your own hearts are not evil and unbelieving, turning you away from the living God. You must warn each other every day, while it is still 'today,' so that none of you will be deceived by sin and hardened against God. For if we are faithful to the end, trusting God just as firmly as when we first believed, we will share in all that belongs to Christ" (NLT).

In the New King James Version of the Bible, verse 14 says, "holding confidently and steadfast till the end." The only way to keep this confidence till the end is by removing any unbelief in our hearts and encouraging each other daily. Believers (Christians) must warn each other every day because there are temptations bombarding us every day. This is why it is important for you to go to church and to have the right friends. Having the right people around you will help you resist some of the sins that you struggle with now. And I hear someone saying, "Well, that is not very Christian to remove my friends, is it?" Sometimes we get attached to people because of things we do whether good or bad. Satan wants you to think that it is mean to get rid of that friend, but in reality, you are removing yourself so that you can become the Christian you need to be.

Some people will want to grow with you and others will want to keep doing the same thing. But as you grow, realize you cannot love God and keep doing the things that displease Him or even be in the company of those who continually dishonor God. When you operate as the person God created you to be, you realize that you were never supposed to be friends with that person in the first place. The question now is, will you trust God for the new friends He will bring?

117

➤ Galatians 6:1: "Dear brothers and sisters, if another believer is overcome by some sin, you who are godly should gently and humbly help that person back onto the right path. And be careful not to fall into the same temptation yourself" (NLT).

Now as you grow stronger in Christ, God may open the door for you to go back and witness to that person. However, you may never go back to that friend, but know that God will open doors for you to help others. The key is being careful to make sure you do not fall back into that temptation.

Let me help make this simple by providing an example from my life. I currently have a friend whose name is Dominique. We have been friends for over 18 plus years. We used to go to 20 and under clubs and go dancing. As we got older, we went to 21 and over clubs and went dancing, and we were always trying to hit on this girl and that girl. We are gentlemen, well-educated, respectful, and great guys; however, I started to really understand what it meant to walk Christianity out, and some of my behavior was not pleasing to God which made us hang out less. When I say walking Christianity out, I mean being led by the Spirit of God and realizing I cannot continue to live by the world's standards, but by God's Holy standards!

There have been some friends in my life that I had to cut out, but Dominique and I are still friends to this day. The difference is, I do not go with him to do the same things we used to do, because God has me in a totally different place spiritually and in ministry. When God has a purpose and calling in your life, you have to move, do, and go where He says. God is everywhere, but He only manifests (shows) His presence when you walk where He is leading! My prayer is that those who God has connected me to will understand more fully the power of Christ in their life and start to walk in it to the fullest, as we all should!

Remember, YOU ARE VICTORIOUS!

➢ Hebrews 10:32-36: "Think back on those early days when you first learned about Christ. Remember how you remained faithful even though it meant terrible suffering. Sometimes you were exposed to public ridicule and were beaten, and sometimes you helped others who were suffering the same things. You suffered along with those who were thrown into jail, and when all you owned was taken from you, you accepted it with joy. You knew there were better things waiting for you that will last forever. So do not throw away this confident trust in the Lord. Remember the great reward it brings you! Patient endurance is what you need now, so that you will continue to do God's will. Then you will receive all that he has promised" (NLT).

These verses let us know that if we keep the confidence, we will receive a great reward: eternal life when Christ returns! I love verse 32 because I want you to know that once you become a Christian and are serious, it will not be easy. There will be struggles because you will be battling the flesh, which you followed for so long.

➢ 2 Corinthians 4:7-10: "We now have this light shining in our hearts, but we ourselves are like fragile clay jars containing this great treasure. This makes it clear that our great power is from God, not from ourselves. We are pressed on every side by troubles, but we are not crushed. We are perplexed, but not driven to despair. We are hunted down, but never abandoned by God. We get knocked down, but we are not destroyed. Through suffering, our bodies continue to share in the death of Jesus so that the life of Jesus may also be seen in our bodies" (NLT).

Some would say, "I do not want to share with Jesus in this way." But Jesus was victorious. Just know that God will never abandon you because He told you that He would never leave you

119

nor forsake you. Understand that even when it does not look like it, you have the victory and the power lies within you, as Ephesians 3:20 said. If you are battling, that is a good thing because you realize what you should be doing even if you slip up a few times (and you will slip up, but God is forgiving).

> 1 John 1:9: "If we confess our sins, He is faithful and just to forgive us *our* sins and to cleanse us from all unrighteousness" (NKJV).

When you are not battling and just doing what is wrong, then you need to be worried. This is when you know you are entangled in a sin and have become numb to it. Remember, victory over this is yours and at this point you must pray and possibly even fast.

The enemy, the devil (Satan), is real and his demons or evil spirits are real, too. The devil will tempt you, but you have the victory to overcome every temptation and God will provide a way out as well.

> James 4:6-8: "And he gives grace generously. As the Scriptures say, 'God opposes the proud but gives grace to the humble.' So humble yourselves before God. Resist the devil, and he will flee from you. Come close to God, and God will come close to you. Wash your hands, you sinners; purify your hearts, for your loyalty is divided between God and the world" (NLT).

> 1 Corinthians 10:13: "No temptation has overtaken you except such as is common to man; but God *is* faithful, who will not allow you to be tempted beyond what you are able, but with the temptation will also make the way of escape, that you may be able to bear *it*" (NKJV).

The key is humility. When you are humble, you hear and submit to God. When you submit to God, you will not listen to the deception of the enemy and he will flee. The humbler you are, the closer you will draw to God and in return, He promises to draw close to you. So endure through the trials and tribulations, because if you do, you will see how good God was while you were in the thick of it, and how He provided a way of escape for you. You will learn to trust God more, which will help you when the next trial comes along.

> Romans 8:37-39: "No, despite all these things, overwhelming victory is ours through Christ, who loved us. And I am convinced that nothing can ever separate us from God's love. Neither death nor life, neither angels nor demons, neither our fears for today nor our worries about tomorrow—not even the powers of hell can separate us from God's love. No power in the sky above or in the earth below—indeed, nothing in all creation will ever be able to separate us from the love of God that is revealed in Christ Jesus our Lord" (NLT).

Again, you have the victory! Nothing can separate what God has done through Jesus. Jesus said, "It is finished." This means when He died, sin's control died, and when He was resurrected, life and blessings were made available for those who are in Christ! It is through our life circumstances that we learn more about God's characteristics.

> James 1:2-5: "My brethren, count it all joy when you fall into various trials, knowing that the testing of your faith produces patience. But let patience have *its* perfect work, that you may be perfect and complete, lacking nothing. If any of you lacks wisdom, let him ask of God, who gives to all liberally and without reproach, and it will be given to him" (NKJV).

You are in a situation now that is bad and has been bad, but do not get weary because your harvest—your reaping—is COMING! Look to God, continue to pray, and be ready to take steps of faith that you have never taken before. Wait on God and be patient, because even though you may not see it right now, God is doing something; if you wait, you will be perfect and complete. Chances are, there is someone else going through the same thing you've endured.  Now you will be able to tell them how you are making it and ultimately give God the glory!

The first example out of the Bible I want to share with you is out of Exodus.

> Exodus 17:8-16: "While the people of Israel were still at Rephidim, the warriors of Amalek attacked them. Moses commanded Joshua, 'Choose some men to go out and fight the army of Amalek for us. Tomorrow, I will stand at the top of the hill, holding the staff of God in my hand.' So Joshua did what Moses had commanded and fought the army of Amalek.  Meanwhile, Moses, Aaron, and Hur climbed to the top of a nearby hill.  As long as Moses held up the staff in his hand, the Israelites had the advantage.  But whenever he dropped his hand, the Amalekites gained the advantage.  Moses' arms soon became so tired he could no longer hold them up.  So Aaron and Hur found a stone for him to sit on.  Then they stood on each side of Moses, holding up his hands.  So his hands held steady until sunset.  As a result, Joshua overwhelmed the army of Amalek in battle.  After the victory, the LORD instructed Moses, 'Write this down on a scroll as a permanent reminder, and read it aloud to Joshua: I will erase the memory of Amalek from under heaven.'  Moses built an altar there and named it Yahweh-Nissi (which means 'the LORD is my banner').  He said, 'They have raised their fist against the LORD'S throne, so now the LORD will be at war with Amalek generation after generation'" (NLT).

In these verses, you see how important it is to have people on your side who believe the same thing you do.  Moses goes on the hill with two people who know that if God did not help, they could not win.  Moses knew God would be with Him because He told him.

> Exodus 3:12: "God answered, 'I will be with you. And this is your sign that I am the one who has sent you:

When you have brought the people out of Egypt, you will worship God at this very mountain'" (NLT).

When you are in a fight, you must know that God is with you, that you must look to the hills from where your help comes (as Psalm 121:1-2 says in NKJV), and that even though you must take action and move, it is God who is winning the battle for you. You can have this same kind of victory if you would just look to God to help you fight your battles. Just as Moses was equipped with the rod of God, we are equipped with spiritual weapons found in Ephesians 6 starting at verse 10. A few of these weapons are the sword of the Spirit, which is the word of God and the shield of faith to stop the fiery arrows of the devil.

> Proverbs 18:21: "Death and life are in the power of the tongue, and those who love it *and* indulge it will eat its fruit *and* bear the consequences of their words" (AMP).

God spoke the world into existence, and if you are saved, the living God lives in you in the person of the Holy Spirit. Because of this, you have authority to speak and affect change for good or for bad.

Use your weapons. Lift your hands and praise God that you are connected to the right people like Moses because you will need help on this journey, and watch God move on your behalf in the challenging times you may go through. Just a side note and reminder from earlier: the word "through" indicates movement from one side or point and out another. It can also mean from the beginning to the end or completion. You must realize that if you are going through, that means at some point victory will come and you will be at the end of that situation and you will be more COMPLETE because He is your Savior!

> Isaiah 43:1-2: "But now, O Jacob, listen to the lord who created you. O Israel, the one who formed you says, 'Do not be afraid, for I have ransomed you. I have called you by name; you are mine. When you go through deep waters, I will be with you. When you go through rivers

of difficulty, you will not drown. When you walk through the fire of oppression, you will not be burned up; the flames will not consume you'" (NLT).

➢ Isaiah 43:5-7: "Do not be afraid, for I am with you. I will gather you and your children from east and west. I will say to the north and south, 'Bring my sons and daughters back to Israel from the distant corners of the earth. Bring all who claim me as their God, for I have made them for my glory. It was I who created them'" (NLT).

➢ Isaiah 43:11: "I, yes I, am the Lord, and there is no other Savior" (NLT).

Let's look at the second example out of the Bible.

➢ 2 Chronicles 20:10-23: "'And now see what the armies of Ammon, Moab, and Mount Seir are doing. You would not let our ancestors invade those nations when Israel left Egypt, so they went around them and did not destroy them. Now see how they reward us! For they have come to throw us out of your land, which you gave us as an inheritance. O our God, won't you stop them? We are powerless against this mighty army that is about to attack us. We do not know what to do, but we are looking to you for help.' As all the men of Judah stood before the LORD with their little ones, wives, and children, the Spirit of the LORD came upon one of the men standing there. His name was Jahaziel son of Zechariah, son of Benaiah, son of Jeiel, son of Mattaniah, a Levite who was a descendant of Asaph. He said, 'Listen, all you people of Judah and Jerusalem! Listen, King Jehoshaphat! This is what the LORD says: Do not be afraid! Don't be discouraged by this mighty army, for the battle is not yours, but God's. Tomorrow, march out against them. You will find them coming up through the ascent of Ziz at the end of the valley that opens into the wilderness of Jeruel. But you will not even need to fight. Take your positions; then stand still and watch the LORD'S victory. He is with you, O people of Judah and Jerusalem. Do not be afraid or discouraged. Go out against them tomorrow, for the LORD is with you!' Then King Jehoshaphat bowed low with his face to the ground. And all the people of Judah and Jerusalem did the same, worshiping the LORD. Then the Levites from the clans of Kohath and Korah stood to praise the LORD, the God of Israel, with a very loud shout. Early the next morning the army of Judah went out into the wilderness of Tekoa. On the way Jehoshaphat stopped and said, 'Listen to me, all you people of Judah and Jerusalem! Believe in the LORD your God, and you will be able to stand firm. Believe in his prophets, and you will succeed.' After consulting the people, the king appointed singers to walk ahead of the army, singing to the LORD and praising him for his holy splendor. This is what they sang: 'Give thanks to the LORD; his faithful love endures forever!' At the very moment they began to sing and give praise *[ACTion]*, the LORD caused the armies of Ammon, Moab, and Mount Seir to start fighting among themselves. The armies of Moab and Ammon turned against their allies from Mount Seir and killed every one of them. After they had destroyed the army of Seir, they began attacking each other" (NLT).

The first thing you see is that even though Jehoshaphat had some fear, he still sought the Lord and proclaimed a fast throughout all of Judah (in 2 Chronicles 20:3 in NLT).

➤ Matthew 17:21: "However, this kind does not go out except by prayer and fasting" (NKJV).

Regardless of what situation you will go through in life, you must focus your eyes on God instead of the situation (like in 2 Chronicles 20:12). The more you focus on the situation, the more distracted you are from God's vision for your life. There is tremendous power when a community of believers comes together for one purpose to hear from God. It says that all of Judah fasted and in verse 13 it confirms this. So when we come together for one purpose, you can be assured there is going to be a mighty move of God. In some victories, you are going to need family members, church members, and friends who believe what you do. Make sure you have the right players on your team.

In verses 14 and 15, Jahaziel speaks to Judah as the Spirit of the Lord had told him and says, "The battle is not yours, but God's" (NKJV). As you continue to read in verses 16 and 17, he tells them to go out tomorrow for they will not need to fight in this battle. When you do the right thing and seek God (see Appendix for ideas about fasting), He will answer you and direct you in the way you should go. When He speaks, be obedient, willing, and have faith.

The only way out of the dilemmas you go through are the steps of faith you must take. Think about some of the phrases mentioned above: go out and march, don't fight, but take position. If you heard this, you would be thinking, *Well, if I do not have to fight, why go out?* But faith is being totally obedient even if you do not understand and even if you do not have all the details. When you take a step, God will continue to reveal the rest! Believing that God's promises are true, accepting them, and daring to trust in them, leads to victory—as you will see.

In 2 Chronicles verses 20 through 23 you see that they sang praises and obeyed God, and their enemies were defeated without fighting. At a certain point, your praying and fasting turns into praise. When you know you have heard from God, you can praise because you know you have the victory!

➢ 2 Chronicles 20:24: "So when Judah came to a place overlooking the wilderness, they looked toward the multitude; and there *were* their dead bodies, fallen on the earth. No one had escaped" (NKJV).

➢ Psalm 23:5a: "You prepare a table before me in the presence of my enemies" (NKJV).

➤ Exodus 14:13: "And Moses said to the people, 'Do not be afraid. Stand still, and see the salvation of the Lord, which He will accomplish for you today. For the Egyptians whom you see today, you shall see again no more forever" (NKJV).

➤ Exodus 14:30-31: "So the Lord saved Israel that day out of the hand of the Egyptians, and Israel saw the Egyptians dead on the seashore. Thus Israel saw the great work which the Lord had done in Egypt; so the people feared the Lord, and believed the Lord and His servant Moses" (NKJV).

I am just trying to get everyone to realize that if you trust God— if you stop trying to figure it out and stand on God's word— VICTORY WILL BE YOURS! You have to realize that a lot of times God's plan may not make sense, but if you will just submit and obey, you will see that it will work out and deliverance will come to your situation. Just as the coach may send a play that you do not think will work, you have to trust him and do it anyway. The coach can see things from his position that the players cannot. In the same way, God gives us directions that we may not understand fully, but from His position He can see the defense (the enemy) and knows what will work as long as you execute.

➤ 2 Peter 1:2-4: "Grace and peace be multiplied to you in the knowledge of God and of Jesus our Lord, as His divine power has given to us all things that *pertain* to life and godliness, through the knowledge of Him who called us by glory and virtue, by which have been given to us exceedingly great and precious promises, that through these you may be partakers of the divine nature, having escaped the corruption *that is* in the world through lust" (NKJV).

My prayer is that now you are more complete than when you were on page one. Life will throw you curve balls, but you serve a God who will coach you to hitting a homerun every time!

Enjoy being more complete in Christ! Let this scripture give you strength and encouragement knowing that He will complete what He has begun in you.

> ➢ Philippians 1:6: "And I am certain that God, who began the good work within you, will continue his work until it is finally finished *[complete]* on the day when Christ Jesus returns" (NLT).

## Scripture Glossary

Below are the scripture verses I used in each chapter's "Faith Walk." Reflect back on these if you are struggling in your journey.

NLT – New Living Translation
NKJV – New King James Version
NIV – New International Version
MSG – Message Bible
AMP – Amplified Version
AMPC – Amplified Version, Classic Edition

### Chapter 1
Psalms 34:8-10 NLT
Numbers 23:19 NLT
Psalms 84:11 NLT
Isaiah 55:11 NKJV

### Chapter 2
2 Timothy 2:15 NLT
Psalms 119:105 NLT
Proverbs 3:5-6 NKJV
2 Timothy 3:16 NLT
1 Timothy 4:7-8 NLT
Ephesians 1:3 NLT
Matthew 6:19-21 NLT

### Chapter 3
Genesis 2:15 – 3:24 NLT
Romans 6:23 NLT
Romans 3:23-24 NLT
Romans 10:8-10 NLT

John 3:16-18 NLT
Ephesians 2:8-10 NLT
Romans 8:11 NLT
Ephesians 1:13 NLT
James 3:13-18 NLT
John 14:15-17 NLT
John 16:13-14 NLT
John 14:12-14 NLT
Psalms 139:13-18 NLT
Genesis 1:26-31 NLT
Psalms 8:4-5 NLT
Philippians 4:13 NKJV

### Chapter 4
Psalms 7:9-10 NKJV
Job 1:8 NLT
John 16:33 AMP
Matthew 1:23 NKJV
Job 1:1 AMP
Job 23:10 NLT
Job 42:10 NLT
2 Timothy 2:13 NLT
Isaiah 40:29-31 NKJV
Romans 8:26-27 NLT
Daniel 3:13-20 NLT
Psalms 84:11 NLT
Psalms 91:2-4 NLT
Psalms 34:1 NKJV
Romans 14:8 NKJV
Psalms 37:25 NKJV
Psalms 34:10 NLT
Job 14:14b NKJV
Job 42:5 NKJV

### Chapter 5
Hebrews 12:1-2 NLT
Hebrews 13:8 NKJV

Exodus 20:12 NLT
Matthew 19:19 NKJV
Ephesians 4:29 NLT
Titus 3:2 NLT
1 Corinthians 6:18-20 NLT
Joshua 1:8 AMP
1 Corinthians 3:16-17 MSG
Ephesians 5:15-21 NLT
1 Corinthians 6:9-10 NLT
Galatians 5:19-21 NLT
1 Peter 4:1-3 NIV
Proverbs 8:6-8 NKJV
Proverbs 15:7 NLT
Proverbs 20:19 NLT
Romans 12:2 NLT
Romans 12:9-18 NLT
Proverbs 8:34-35 NKJV
Romans 8:11 NLT
Matthew 28:20 NLT
Hebrews 13:5-6 NLT
Galatians 6:7-10 NLT
Nehemiah 8:10b NKJV
Proverbs 3:5-6 AMP
Ephesians 6:10-18 NLT
John 10:10 NKJV
1 Corinthians 10:13 NKJV
1 Samuel 17:34-39 NKJV
Romans 5:3-5 NLT
James 1:2-4 NLT
1 John 4:4 AMP
Genesis 39:21-23 NLT

**Chapter 6**
John 14:6 NLT
Mark 2:16-17 NKJV
Galatians 5:22-23 NKJV
Romans 12 NLT

1 Corinthians 6:9-11 NLT
Galatians 5:19-21 NLT
Ephesians 5:3-5 NIV
John 15:1-2 NLT
Galatians 5:16-18 NLT
Galatians 5:24-26 NLT
Matthew 22:37-40 NLT
John 13:34 NKJV
John 15:13 NKJV
Philippians 4:13 NKJV
John 14:16-17 NLT
John 14:26 NLT
Matthew 5:43-44 NKJV
Galatians 5:22-23 NLT
Philippians 4:8 NLT
2 Peter 1:5-8 NLT
Psalms 119:11 NKJV

**Chapter 7**
Lamentations 3:22-23 NLT
2 Corinthians 10:3-5 NLT
Romans 7:14-25 NLT
James 1:14-15 NLT
James 4:7-8 NKJV
Matthew 19:26 NKJV
John 15:5 NKJV
Matthew 18:18 AMPC
Matthew 6:10 NKJV
John 14:13-14 NKJV
2 Corinthians 2:11 NKJV
Matthew 6:14-15 NLT
Jeremiah 1:5 NLT
Jeremiah 29:11 NKJV
Psalms 139:13-18 NLT
Matthew 7:7-11 NLT
1 John 5:14-15 NKJV
James 1:5 NIV

Isaiah 43:18-19 NLT
Proverbs 4:23 NIV
Matthew 12:33-35 NLT
Colossians 3:1-2 NLT
James 1:16-17 NLT
1 Timothy 4:7-8 NLT
Proverbs 2:6 AMPC
Hebrews 13:8 NLT
Psalms 1:1-3 NLT
1 Corinthians 2:14 NLT
1 Corinthians 3:5-7 NLT
Proverbs 3:5-6 AMPC
James 1:2-4 NLT
Proverbs 3:5-6 AMP
Psalms 119:11 NKJV
Proverbs 4:4 NKJV
Proverbs 4:20-23 NLT
Psalms 51:10 NKJV
Philippians 4:19 NKJV
Ephesians 3:20 NIV
Mark 16:17-18 NLT
Revelations 3:15-16 NLT
Acts 13:22 NLT
2 Corinthians 4:16-18 NKJV
Ephesians 1:3 NKJV
1 Corinthians 2:9 NLT
Exodus 13:21-22 NLT
Joshua 1:5 NKJV
John 16:12-15 NKJV
John 14:10-11 NKJV
1 Corinthians 2:10-14 NKJV
Zechariah 4:6 NKJV
Matthew 7:7-11 NLT
Psalms 91:1-2, 9-13 NLT
Psalms 27:5 NIV
Psalms 31:20 NIV
Colossians 1:27 NIV

Matthew 18:19-20 NLT

**Chapter 8**
1 Samuel 30:6-8, 16-20 NLT
1 Corinthians 15:57 NLT
1 John 5:4-5 NLT
John 16:33 AMP
Hebrews 11:1, 6 NKJV
Isaiah 26:3 AMP
2 Timothy 1:7 NKJV
1 John 4:4 AMP
Nehemiah 8:10b NKJV
Ephesians 3:20 NLT
Psalms 34:8 NKJV
Hebrews 3:12-14 NLT
Galatians 6:1 NLT
Hebrews 10:32-36 NLT
2 Corinthians 4:7-10 NLT
1 John 1:9 NKJV
James 4:6-8 NLT
1 Corinthians 10:13 NKJV
Romans 8:37-39 NLT
James 1:2-5 NKJV
Exodus 17:8-16 NLT
Exodus 3:12 NLT
Psalms 121:1-2 NKJV
Proverbs 18:21 AMP
Isaiah 43:1-2, 5-7, 11 NLT
2 Chronicles 20:10-23 NLT
2 Chronicles 20:3 NLT
Matthew 17:21 NKJV
2 Chronicles 20:24 NKJV
Psalms 23:5a NKJV
Exodus 14:13, 30-31 NKJV
2 Peter 1:2-4 NKJV
Philippians 1:6 NLT

# APPENDIX

## A. SONG

The song, "The Best in Me" by Marvin Sapp truly details how God feels about you, regardless of what anyone has told you. You must believe and know that God sees the best in you because He made everyone in his image and likeness. Now you must read the word of God so that as you learn about God and who He is, you will realize how wonderful you are and the kind of power you have because of Jesus Christ dying and being resurrected for you. If a coach, parent, teacher, or anyone says you are no one, do not believe that, but BELIEVE GOD who created you, NOT THEM. One of the lyrics is, "He saw the best in me, when everyone else around could only see the worst in me." Be sure to look this song up!

## B. Dictionary of Christian Words

In this section I have listed some definitions for further understanding and have attached scripture at the end so that you can see where this can be found in the bible. These definitions are my own words combined with the Holman Bible Dictionary as a reference.

1. Mercy – not getting what you deserve; God's compassion and kindness. (Ephesians 2:3-5)
2. Grace – getting what you do not deserve; God's unearned favor. (Ephesians 2:8-9)
3. Blessed – to cause to prosper, to make happy. (Romans 4:5-8, Matthew 5:1-12)
4. Kingdom of God – the reign or rule of God extended to us through the ministry of Jesus. It is not a location or place, but about God being first in your life. (Matthew 6:33, Mark 1:15)
5. Righteousness – a person who has accepted Jesus is looked at by God as being free from the guilt of sin. (2 Corinthians 5:21)
6. Fasting – laying aside of food (or other things) for a period of time when the believer is seeking to know God in a deeper way. Denying wants and needs and replacing them with God's word and prayer. This is done to hear from God, not to get God's blessing. (Matthew 6:16-18, Daniel 9:3)
7. Justification – when an individual is brought into an undeserving, right relationship with God and ever sin is acquitted (not guilty) through the death and resurrection of Christ. (Romans 3:21-26)
8. Sanctification – this comes after justification. It is the process of being made holy or set apart, resulting in a changed lifestyle. (1 Corinthians 6:11)
9. Glorification – The point when Jesus returns and we are called to live with Him in our spiritual bodies. (Romans 8:17-18, 23)

10. Glory – the weight that accompanies God's presence. A form of excellence which brings praise and amazement. (Exodus 16:10, Exodus 24:17, Exodus 33:18-23)

11. Lord and Savior – Lord means Jesus is our master, owner, King, and supreme authority. Savior means Jesus died for our sins so we could live a life free of guilt/condemnation and to have a right relationship with Him now that we may live with Him forever when He comes back. (Philippians 2:9-11, Romans 10:9)

12. Atonement – to make up for a wrong act by a sacrificial offering. Sin separated us from God, but Jesus' death on the cross made up for our sins. (2 Corinthians 5:18-19, Hebrews 9:22)

13. Reconciliation – Due to Jesus' life, death, and resurrection, we are no longer enemies but friends of God. God and people are brought back together in fellowship/harmony again and now we have peace with God. (Romans 5:10-11)

14. Redeemed – to buy freedom. Because of Jesus' death, he paid the price to buy us back and set us free from our slavery to sin. He rescued and ransomed us. (Colossians 1:13-14)

## C. Daniel Fast Food Guide

Fasting is done to develop a closer relationship with God by denying the things of the world and focusing more on Christ. First and foremost, fasting does not have to be from food. This is just one way. Other options are from technology, social media, TV, or drinks. While fasting, it is vital to be in the Word and prayer even more so that you can hear from God and strengthen this discipline.

When doing a Daniel Fast please make sure to **READ THE LABEL** when purchasing packaged, canned, or bottled foods. They should be **sugar-free** and **chemical-free**. Keep this in mind as you review this list of acceptable foods.

**Foods to include in your diet during the Daniel Fast**
All fruits: These can be fresh, frozen, dried, juiced, or canned. Fruits include but are not limited to apples, apricots, bananas, blackberries, blueberries, boysenberries, cantaloupe, cherries, cranberries, figs, grapefruit, grapes, guava, honeydew melon, kiwi, lemons, limes, mangoes, nectarines, oranges, papayas, peaches, pears, pineapples, plums, prunes, raisins, raspberries, strawberries, tangelos, tangerines, and watermelon.
All vegetables: These can be fresh, frozen, dried, juiced, or canned. Vegetables include but are not limited to artichokes, asparagus, beets, broccoli, Brussels sprouts, cabbage, carrots, cauliflower, celery, chili peppers, collard greens, corn, cucumbers, eggplant, garlic, ginger root, kale, leeks, lettuce, mushrooms, mustard greens, okra, onions, parsley, potatoes, radishes, rutabagas, scallions, spinach, sprouts, squashes, sweet potatoes, tomatoes, turnips, watercress, yams, and zucchini. Veggie burgers are an option if you are not allergic to soy.

All whole grains: Including but not limited to whole wheat, brown rice, millet, quinoa, oats, barley, grits, whole wheat pasta, whole wheat tortillas, rice cakes, and popcorn.

All nuts and seeds: Including but not limited to sunflower seeds, cashews, peanuts, and sesame. Nut butters including peanut butter are also included.

All legumes: These can be canned or dried. Legumes include but are not limited to dried beans, pinto beans, split peas, lentils, black eyed peas, kidney beans, black beans, cannellini beans, and white beans.

All quality oils: Including but not limited to olive, canola, grape seed, peanut, and sesame.

Beverages: Spring water, distilled water, or other pure waters.

Other: Tofu, soy products, vinegar, seasonings, salt, herbs, and spices.

**Foods to avoid on the Daniel Fast**

All meat and animal products: Including but not limited to beef, lamb, pork, poultry, and fish.

All dairy products: Including but not limited to milk, cheese, cream, butter, and eggs.

All sweeteners: Including but not limited to sugar, raw sugar, honey, syrups, molasses, and cane juice.

All leavened bread: Including Ezekiel Bread (it contains yeast and honey) and baked goods.

All refined and processed food products: Including but not limited to artificial flavorings, food additives, chemicals, white rice, white flour, and foods that contain artificial preservatives.

All deep-fried foods: Including but not limited to potato chips, French fries, and corn chips.

All solid fats: Including shortening, margarine, lard, and foods high in fat.

Beverages: Including but not limited to coffee, tea, herbal teas, carbonated beverages, energy drinks, and alcohol.

Remember, **READ THE LABELS!**

## D. Names of God

These names are important because they describe who God is. We worship God not for what He does, but simply because of who He is. Everything I need is wrapped up in Him! We learn a lot about God's character through our trials and personal experiences. Through His word, I knew that God was a provider, but when I am lacking and God provides, I know for myself with a firsthand account. The names below can be found in *The Names of God* by Ken Hemphill (2001), or in the scripture I have listed.

1. Jehovah Jireh – The Lord will provide (Genesis 22:14)
2. Jehovah Rophe – The Lord that heals (Exodus 15:26)
3. Jehovah Nissi – The Lord our banner; victory (Exodus 17:15)
4. Jehovah Shalom – The Lord is peace (Judges 6:24)
5. Jehovah Rohi – The Lord my shepherd (Psalm 23:1)
6. Jehovah Shammah – The Lord is there (Ezekiel 48:35)
7. Jehovah Mekadesh – The Lord who sanctifies you (Exodus 31:13)
8. Jehovah Tsidkenu – The Lord our righteousness (Jeremiah 23:5-6, Jeremiah 33:16)

## OTHER BOOK RESOURCES

- ➤ *Jesus Is Student Edition: Discovering Who He Is Changes Who You Are* by Judah Smith
- ➤ *The Prayer of Jesus: The Promise and Power of Living in the Lord's Prayer* by Ken Hemphill
- ➤ *Doing Right in a Wrong World* by Darryl S. Brister
- ➤ *The Power of Persistent Prayer: Praying With Greater Purpose and Passion* by Cindy Jacobs
- ➤ *The Prayer Dare: Take the Challenge That Will Transform Your Relationship With God* by Ron Kincaid
- ➤ *What the Bible is All About* by Dr. Henrietta C. Mears
- ➤ *Holman Bible Dictionary*

# About THE Author

Justin Campbell is a devoted man of God who understands he is just an earthen vessel being used by God. Justin is a member of Canaan Christian Church in Louisville, KY, where he is a Bible study teacher on Wednesdays and serves over the Fellowship of Christian Athletes at New Albany High School in Indiana. He and his wife, Tinika, also have a marriage ministry. They have two kids, Jada and Mariah, and a stepdaughter Ashlee, who are all wonderful!

Justin has been called on by churches, schools, and others to speak to youth and adults. He loves being able to allow God to use him to be a blessing to those in attendance, because he understands he has been appointed by God and someone will be blessed. God has also gifted Justin to write Christian posts for social media purposes. Once he reaches 365 posts, he plans to publish a 365-day devotional.

At the end of the day, Justin just wants to be used to glorify God. He spends much of his time immersed in the word of God, in prayer, and reading Christian books. He is not perfect by any means, but he understands, like Paul, that it is all about the grace and mercy of God. Like David, he is a man after God's own heart! Justin wholeheartedly believes in the authority that has been given to him and is not afraid to speak what the Holy Spirit has provided him.

If you wish to contact Justin, visit his website: www.justin-campbell.com